TEACHING TO INDIVIDUAL DIFFERENCES IN SCIENCE AND ENGINEERING LIBRARIANSHIP

T0383232

TEACHING TO INDIVIDUAL DIFFERENCES IN SCIENCE AND ENGINEERING LIBRARIANSHIP

Adapting Library Instruction to Learning Styles and Personality Characteristics

JEANINE M. WILLIAMSON

CHANDOS
PUBLISHING
An imprint of Elsevier

Chandos Publishing is an imprint of Elsevier
50 Hampshire Street, 5th Floor, Cambridge, MA 02139, United States
The Boulevard, Langford Lane, Kidlington, OX5 1GB, United Kingdom

Notices
Knowledge and best practice in this field are constantly changing. As new research and
experience broaden our understanding, changes in research methods, professional practices,
or medical treatment may become necessary.

Practitioners and researchers must always rely on their own experience and knowledge
in evaluating and using any information, methods, compounds, or experiments described
herein. In using such information or methods they should be mindful of their own safety
and the safety of others, including parties for whom they have a professional responsibility.

To the fullest extent of the law, neither the Publisher nor the authors, contributors, or
editors, assume any liability for any injury and/or damage to persons or property as a
matter of products liability, negligence or otherwise, or from any use or operation of any
methods, products, instructions, or ideas contained in the material herein.

Library of Congress Cataloging-in-Publication Data
A catalog record for this book is available from the Library of Congress

British Library Cataloguing-in-Publication Data
A catalogue record for this book is available from the British Library

ISBN: 978-0-08-101881-1(print)
ISBN: 978-0-08-101882-8 (online)

For information on all Chandos publications visit our
website at https://www.elsevier.com/books-and-journals

Working together
to grow libraries in
developing countries

www.elsevier.com • www.bookaid.org

Publisher: Glyn Jones
Acquisition Editor: Glyn Jones
Editorial Project Manager: Thomas Van Der Ploeg
Production Project Manager: Debasish Ghosh
Cover Designer: Victoria Esser Pearson

Typeset by SPi Global, India

CONTENTS

PREFACE

Learning is an interplay of people and content. It is influenced by characteristics of the teacher, the students, and the subject matter. Examples of teacher characteristics that may influence student learning include the teacher's level of anxiety, his or her communication skills, knowledge, preparation, and warmth. Students may be affected by their abstract problem-solving ability, their interests, their attentiveness, mood, energy, or any number of additional characteristics. Subject matter characteristics obviously influence the learning experience. For example, does the content involve social interaction, technical understanding, thinking, doing, and so forth? All of these subject-matter requirements interact with student and teacher characteristics to produce learning (or nonlearning)!

The science or engineering librarian is also affected by the context in which he or she teaches. Does he or she only have the opportunity to interact with students in a "one-shot" class? How big are the classes? Obviously a 100-student lecture class may introduce elements into the instruction that a 10-person graduate seminar does not. Has the class instructor provided an assignment to motivate students to engage with library instruction? Have the students met the librarian before encountering him or her in the library instruction setting? Have the students ever used library services before? Are they aware that there are search resources available beyond Google?

This book will prompt science and engineering librarians to consider how to incorporate individual differences (i.e., characteristics of teachers and students) into their teaching. It will describe two kinds of individual differences, personality traits and learning styles,[1] and explain how these are likely to impact learning and instruction. Along the way, the book keeps in the forefront how the subject matter (science or engineering content) and the instructional context interact with these individual differences.

Because personalizing instruction to individual differences is not without controversy, the book will also examine how matching instruction to individual differences (particularly learning styles) has been challenged. Whether or not the reader comes away with the belief that "tailoring" instruction to personality or learning styles would be beneficial, he or she will learn about the importance of individual differences in teaching and learning.

---

[1] Specifically, the Kolb model of learning styles is used. There will be more about that choice later.

STRUCTURE OF THE BOOK

Chapter 1 defines individual differences as characteristics that vary across a group of people. I explain that learning styles and personality traits are examples of individual differences that can make a difference in learning and teaching, I review the evidence that college majors and occupations attract and/or retain individuals that have similar personality traits, and individuals' learning styles become accentuated by progressing through a major and working in an occupation.

Chapter 2 presents Kolb's learning styles theory (Kolb, 2015), which states that learning styles are associated with preferences for the four parts of the "learning cycle." I describe Kolb's learning styles and then give examples of how the theory has been applied by engineering educators.

Chapter 3 defines personality traits and explains some ways that personality is related to teaching and learning. The two personality models used in this book are introduced: the 16PF (Conn & Rieke, 1994) and the Big Five/Narrow frameworks (Lounsbury et al., 2003).

Chapter 4 presents extant research on the Kolb learning styles framework and 16PF and Big Five/Narrow personality traits of scientists, engineers, and librarians. In addition, I present research on learning styles and personality trait in diverse populations.

Chapter 5 considers arguments for matching instruction to the personality and learning style characteristics of students. One approach to this kind of personalization is to try to appeal to multiple learning styles or personality traits within a class. Another approach is to appeal to the predominant learning styles or personality traits of the group. A third approach is to try to assess informally the personality characteristics and learning styles of students.

Chapter 6 discusses cases when it is best *not* to match instruction to personality and learning style characteristics. First, I review research evidence not supporting matching instruction to learning styles. Then I point out that mismatches between student characteristics and instruction can sometimes be beneficial, in providing "growth experiences" for the student. Similarly, mismatches between teacher characteristics and student characteristics can sometimes provide incentives for librarians to improve their instruction. At times it may also be best to match instructional methods to the content, rather than individual characteristics.

Chapter 7 reports on a survey of science and engineering librarians' attitudes towards personalization of instruction to personality traits and learning styles. I report on unfavorable and favorable responses to personalization and show how librarians rated themselves, scientists, and engineers on 10 personality traits and 4 learning preferences.

Chapter 8 applies the concepts introduced in the preceding chapters to science and engineering library instruction. I describe opportunities for personalization to personality traits and learning styles within different types of classes. These include introductory science and engineering library classes, science and engineering graduate classes, engineering design classes, and online classes.

Chapter 9 discusses the use of self-reflection about personality traits to improve one's instruction. An example report from a Big Five personality instrument, the IPIP NEO, is given, and the librarian's likely strengths and weaknesses in respect to instruction are summarized. I also include the use of personality and learning styles frameworks in critiquing examples of my own instruction.

Chapter 10 discusses the relevance of personality traits to ABET engineering accreditation standard Criterion 3 and the ACRL Information Literacy Framework for Higher Education of 2015. I show that the skills called for by the two documents are congruous with particular personality traits. I compare and contrast the personality traits aligned with the two documents.

Chapter 11 wraps up the book, discussing practical considerations about adapting instruction to learning styles and personality characteristics. I discuss implications for the future of teaching to individual differences in science and engineering librarianship. I also summarize my view that individual difference models can furnish useful frameworks for instructional design.

REFERENCES

Conn, S. R., & Rieke, M. L. 1994. *16PF fifth edition technical manual*. Champaign, IL: Institute for Personality and Ability Testing.

Kolb, D. A. 2015. *Experiential learning: Experience as the source of learning and development* (2nd ed.). Upper Saddle River, NJ: Pearson Education Ltd.

Lounsbury, J. W., Loveland, J. M., Sundstrom, E. D., Gibson, L. W., Drost, A. W., & Hamrick, F. L. (2003). An investigation of personality traits in relation to career satisfaction. *Journal of Career Assessment, 11*(3), 287–307. http://dx.doi.org/10.1177/1069072703254501.

ACKNOWLEDGMENTS

Thanks to all the people who have supported me in the writing of this book:

George Knott, Glyn Jones, and Thomas Van Der Ploeg at Chandos.

Family Members: Chris Williamson, Mary Williamson, and Will Fletcher.

Colleagues and Mentors: John Lounsbury, Lana Dixon, Peter Fernandez, Ann Viera, Melanie Allen, Donna Braquet, Teresa Berry, Greg March, Kenya Flash, Anna Sandelli, and Teresa Walker.

Also, thanks to Alice Y. Kolb for kindly giving me permission to use descriptions of the nine learning styles in the Kolb Learning Style Inventory 4.0, and Bernice McCarthy for valuable advice on using 4MAT.

CHAPTER 1

Individual Differences

1.1 DEFINITIONS OF INDIVIDUAL DIFFERENCES

Definitions of individual differences point out the reality of traits that distinguish individuals. For example, *The Encyclopedia of Social Psychology* (Baumeister & Vohs, 2007) defines individual differences in terms of enduring psychological characteristics.

Individual differences are the more-or-less enduring psychological characteristics that distinguish one person from another and thus help to define each person's individuality. Among the most important kinds of individual differences are intelligence, personality traits, and values. The study of individual differences is called differential or trait psychology and is more commonly the concern of personality psychologists than social psychologists. Individual differences are neither a fiction nor a nuisance; they are enduring psychological features that contribute to the shaping of behavior and to each individual's sense of self. Both social and applied psychology can benefit by taking these enduring dispositions into account.

The Sage Glossary of the Social and Behavioral Sciences (Sullivan, 2009) has a definition of individual differences that is particularly geared to learning.

How individuals differ in traits such as skills, aptitudes, and abilities to learn and perform. Learners may vary in their personalities, motivations, and attributions for their successes and failures when learning—all of which may affect how and why they learn. Additionally, they differ in their preferences for learning and their willingness to learn. Some traits may be more adaptive, whereas others are stable and less malleable, or resistant to change, especially as an individual matures to adulthood. Examples of stable traits are gender, culture, and race. Even education and age are considered as stable traits. Traits that may be more malleable, or adaptive, could include effort and attributions of success and failure, among others. Individual differences may be considered in making the learning environment educationally appropriate, interesting, and relevant.

A theme that typifies most definitions of individual differences is that individual differences vary across people and thus distinguish individuals from one another. As the second definition demonstrates, individual differences are sometimes malleable. As I discuss later, personality traits are considered

Teaching to Individual Differences in Science and Engineering Librarianship
http://dx.doi.org/10.1016/B978-0-08-101881-1.00001-7
1

less malleable than learning styles. Nevertheless, both are examples of differences that vary across people and distinguish individuals from one another.

It is also important to note that when scoring individual difference variables such as personality traits and learning styles, the scores can be averaged for a group of people. For example, one could calculate the Introversion of a sample of engineers. One might want to do this to ascertain the characteristics of a "typical" engineer, while recognizing that individual engineers will differ in respect to these characteristics.

1.2 IMPORTANCE OF LEARNING STYLES AND PERSONALITY CHARACTERISTICS

Learning style instruments[2] and personality tests used in academic psychology often measure traits along a range. For example, questions about Extraversion on "Big Five" personality instruments[3] ask respondents to choose options on a Likert scale to indicate how much they agree with each statement. Then these responses are averaged together to give an overall score for the individual on Extraversion. To determine if the score is high, low, or average, the score is compared against the *norms*. Norms are the average values for large, diverse groups of people that are the reference group used in developing and validating the personality test.

Because individuals can score anywhere along the range in relation to the norm group, the scales used in learning style instruments and personality tests can distinguish individuals. To qualify as important individual differences; however, personality traits and learning styles must yield *meaningful* differences. Why might learning styles and personality traits be important individual differences? While answers to this question are developed further in the chapters that follow, I would like to give some concrete examples here.

1.2.1 Learning Styles

Here is an example from my personal experience. I have been fascinated with typologies of human behavior and individual differences since college, and I take "tests" of these characteristics at any chance I get. I took the Kolb Learning Style Instrument (2013) and discovered that my scores fell into the "Analyzing" type. While I realized that I might not *always* prefer to

---

[2]The Kolb Learning Style Instrument (2013) measures values for two scales and then plots the individual's score in four quadrants. Depending on the combination of scores, the individual is placed into one of nine types. See Chapter 2.

[3]The Big Five personality framework, or Five Factor Model, is discussed in Chapter 3.

learn in the ways that this type does, I recognized that this was an approach I typically used.

*If **Analyzing** is your learning style, you are best at taking in a wide range of information and putting it into concise, logical form. You probably are less focused on people and more interested in abstract ideas and concepts.*

I also learned that my learning flexibility was low, which meant that I was fairly consistent in the use of the Analyzing learning style. As I reflected on these results, I realized that my instructional style was similar to this learning style: I most preferred to teach about concepts in a lecture format. When I became aware that learning styles vary widely among individuals, I began to change up my instructional style, incorporating more concrete examples, active exercises, and personal engagement. This improved my teaching.

This is but one example of the significance of learning styles as an individual differences variable. Knowing my learning style encouraged me to vary my teaching style, which made it more effective.

1.2.2 Personality Characteristics

Personality traits are also meaningful individual differences variables when it comes to learning and teaching. Most people are aware from their personal experience that individuals' personalities differ from one another; a very obvious difference is Introversion/Extraversion. Some people are more talkative, active, and outward-focused than others, who may be more reflective, quiet, and inward-focused. Introversion/Extraversion is evident in a wide range of behavior, and it is not surprising that it would be important in learning and teaching situations, as well. For example, as a highly introverted person, I found that teaching (a typically outward-focused behavior) can be challenging and energy-draining at times. When I began teaching, I initially enjoyed teaching individuals or small groups much more than classes.

Similarly, one can readily think of examples where students' personality traits would contribute to their learning behavior. For example, a highly Extraverted student might enjoy group work more than a highly introverted student. A student who is highly reactive (low in emotional stability) might experience more anxiety during learning situations than a calmer student who is high in emotional stability.

1.3 ALIGNMENT BETWEEN LEARNING STYLES, PERSONALITY, DEGREES, AND CAREERS

Two theories explain how learning styles and personality characteristics tend to be aligned with majors and careers. One is a psychological theory, the Holland theory of Person-Environment Fit (Holland, 1973, 1997), which discusses how personality traits tend to be aligned with career and educational choices. Similarly, Kolb discusses why learning styles tend to be aligned with majors and occupations (while recognizing that this is not always the case).

1.3.1 Holland

Holland's Person-Environment Fit theory continues to be widely cited (about 1200 citations in Web of Science to his 1997 3rd edition of *Making Vocational Choices* as of March 2016). Adaptations to the general idea of person-environment fit have been proposed (e.g., Walsh, Craik, & Price, 2000), but Holland's theory is still a widely accepted explanation of how people's personalities, vocational choices, and educational specializations tend to be similar.

Holland viewed both personalities and environments (such as occupational environments) as corresponding to six ideal types, Realistic, Investigative, Artistic, Social, Enterprising, and Conventional.

> *Each type is the product of a characteristic interaction among a variety of cultural and personal forces including peers, biological heredity, parents, social class, culture, and the physical environment. Out of this experience, a person learns first to prefer some activities as opposed to others. Later these activities become strong interests; such interests lead to a special group of competencies. Finally a person's interests and competencies create a particular personal disposition that leads him or her to think, perceive, and act in special ways. (1985, p. 2)*

This developed disposition, in Holland's view, would lead a person to choose occupations corresponding to his or her personality type. For example, a Social person who is friendly and social would tend to select a Social career such as teaching, social work, or the ministry. Holland's theory also applies to choice of college majors.

While Holland's personality types are not discussed at length in this book, his general idea that a person's personality and environment tend to be similar is important. It aligns with empirical findings that there are differences between people in different college majors in respect to Big Five personality traits, for example. A recent systematic review that analyzed differences among students in various college majors from 12 studies (Vedel, 2016) found, among other things, that science majors tended to score lower on Extraversion than economics, law, political science, and medicine majors. The review was based on a combined sample of 13,389 students.

1.3.2 Kolb

Kolb, whose framework is discussed in detail in subsequent chapters (2015), similarly found that there were correspondences between learning styles types and majors and occupations. Kolb drew parallels between the kinds of knowledge studied in different disciplines and learning styles. For example, Kolb found that "hard applied" disciplines such as engineering were associated with the Converging learning style (which combines Abstract Conceptualization and Active Experimentation). Kolb stated that learning styles tended to become accentuated in academic specializations, leading to increasing homogeneity within majors and disciplines. On the other hand, he also gave examples of how learning styles could change as one progressed in an occupation. For example, he discussed the fact that an engineer who becomes a manager often changes in learning style as he or she has to learn to deal with personnel issues.

1.3.3 Retention in College Major and Personality

According to Holland (1985), students tend to leave educational environments that are incongruous with their personalities. One example of an educational environment is the area of academic specialization (the major). Students also tend to respond positively to teachers with similar personalities and levels of intelligence. Holland's theory applies not only to the six personality types and their subtypes that he describes, but also other personality frameworks.

To give but one example, Rosati (1993) found that freshmen engineers having the Myers-Briggs type, ESFP (Extraverted, Sensing, Feeling, Perceiving) were least likely to be retained. The type that was most likely to succeed was INTJ, the opposite of ESFP on the MBTI poles. While the MBTI is not used in this book, these results nevertheless show that students with incongruent personalities may leave engineering.

Similarly Allen and Robbins (2008) found that fit between students' majors and their interests in areas focused on (Data vs Ideas or Things vs People) was a predictor of major persistence. Scores on the Data/Ideas and Things/People interest dimensions are calculated from Holland personality types scores. Allen and Robbins' study used data for nearly 50,000 students from the ACT, which measures students' scores on the six Holland personality/interest types.

Allen and Robbins computed the overall Data/Ideas and Things/People interest scores for major groups such as engineering and then measured relationships between students' fit with the interest scores and their persistence with their major or related majors in their junior year. This study used complex statistical techniques, with the overall finding demonstrating that person-environment fit predicts major persistence.

Differences in students' personality traits across academic specialization also point to the fact that students often tend to be attracted to congruous educational environments. For example, students in medicine tend to be more Extraverted than students in political science and the sciences, but not psychology (Vedel, 2016). Physicians often need to interact with patients and high Extraversion would be helpful for these interactions. Similarly, engineering students score lower on the Big Five trait of Agreeableness than do Counseling and guidance students (Vedel, 2016). This is not surprising since Agreeableness (warmth and collaborativeness) would be more useful for counseling and guidance students, who must learn skills of empathetic listening and encouraging those in distress.

Moses et al. (2011) found that high scores on the Big Five personality factor Openness and low scores on Neuroticism were associated with retention of 129 freshman engineers. Haemmerlie and Montgomery (2012) administered the Hogan Personality Inventory to 755 male and 170 female engineers at a science and technical college and found that low Prudence (analogous to the Big Five factor, Conscientiousness) and high Sociability (analogous to Extraversion) contributed to nonretention of male engineering students. One could see that the traits of Openness, Conscientiousness, and Introversion might be beneficial to engineering students, who must be open to new learning (Openness), reliable, systematic, and organized in problem-solving (Conscientiousness), and focused, with a high level of concentration (Introversion).

Vedel's comprehensive review of Big Five personality trait differences between students of various academic majors (2016) found that engineering students scored lower on Openness than humanities students, political and social science students, and psychology and pedagogical science students. At the same time they were more Conscientious than humanities students and psychology and pedagogical science students. There were no differences in Extraversion among engineering and the other disciplines in Vedel's article.

High Conscientiousness and Openness contributed positively to course grades among 175 students from an instructor's psychology class over 5 years (Lounsbury, Sundstrom, Loveland, & Gibson, 2003). Also, intention to withdraw from college was associated with low values of emotional stability, agreeableness, extraversion, and conscientious (Gibson, Lounsbury, & Saudargas, 2004).

1.3.4 Accentuation of Learning Styles Within College Majors

Kolb and Kolb (2013) plotted educational specializations of students along two dimensions, Concrete Experience/Abstract Conceptualization and Reflective Observation/Active Experimentation.[4] They found that computer and information science majors tended to be abstract and reflective, whereas engineering majors tended to be abstract and active. In comparison with other majors, psychology majors and fine arts majors tended to be more concrete and reflective. These results show that there are differences among the disciplines with respect to learning styles. Also the process of accentuation tends to make academic specializations more homogeneous in respect to students' learning styles.

Kolb (D.A. Kolb, 2015) explained in his exposition of experiential learning theory that students' choice dispositions lead them to choose educational experiences that match these dispositions. Socialization experiences in the academic specialization then reinforce these choice dispositions. Kolb cites a study of physics majors, which showed that students who did not match the discipline's predominantly Convergent learning style (preferring Abstract Conceptualization and Active Experimentation) tended to leave physics, whereas the Convergent students tended to take more physics classes.

Thus, the processes of accentuation of learning styles and person-environment fit contribute to a degree of homogeneity among individuals in academic specializations. While there are individual differences with respect to personality traits and learning styles in any group, one would expect the students in engineering to be more like each other than students in dissimilar disciplines.

1.3.5 Choice of Career and Personality Traits

Due to the same process of person-environment fit, individuals tend to select careers congruous with their personalities and to be more satisfied with, and stay, in congruous careers.

Gottfredson and Holland (1996) classified occupations by their similarity to the Holland personality and environment types, Realistic, Investigative, Artistic, Social, Enterprising, and Conventional. They assigned codes to occupations: for example, Investigative (I) and Realistic (R) were assigned to many engineering specialties. Similarly, Harmon et al. published the

---

[4]These dimensions are discussed more in the chapter on Kolb learning styles.

empirically measured personality/interest preferences of individuals from different occupations who took the Strong Interest Inventory. Conn and Rieke (1994) reported on 16PF personality profiles of individuals in certain occupations, such as engineers and scientists. They also mapped 16PF profiles to Holland types. Lounsbury, Loveland, et al. found differences among members of occupations with his Big Five/Narrow trait instrument, the Personal Style Inventory (2003).

1.3.6 Changes in Personality Traits

Although personality traits such as the Big Five traits of Neuroticism, Extraversion, Openness, Agreeableness, and Conscientiousness change over the lifespan, the overall ranking on traits among individuals tends to remain approximately the same (Lerner, Easterbrooks, & Mistry, 2013). For example, almost everybody becomes more emotionally stable as they age, but the same people who were more emotionally stable than others at a younger age remain more emotionally stable than them at a later age. Thus throughout the lifespan one would expect the mean differences between scientists, engineers and members of norm groups on these traits to be in the same direction. Learning styles can be malleable, reflecting preferences for learning dimensions at different points in time and undergoing accentuation or other changes dependent on learning experiences.

1.3.7 Changes in Learning Styles in Careers

Kolb found that the learning styles of individuals in occupations tended to resemble those of students in the discipline (2015). However, because learning styles are considered more flexible than personality traits, learning styles change as a person progresses in his or her career. I have already mentioned the case of engineering managers, who score higher on the concrete learning style dimension than engineers without responsibility for managing people.

1.4 CONCLUSION

Personality traits and learning styles are meaningful individual differences that intersect with and contribute to the learning process. Because these differences influence individuals' attraction to, and/or retention in, congruent majors and careers, the average values for scientists or engineers give useful information about "typical" science and engineering students. Clearly the typical traits are not the only story, since there is diversity in any group, but these typical traits allow instructors to predict the predominant personality traits and learning style preferences among the students they encounter.

If engineering and sciences students as group have particular personality and learning styles "profiles," then these profiles can inform library instruction although one must always keep in mind that there will be students who do not fit these profiles. As a later chapter shows, engineers and scientists have different personality trait and learning styles profiles from other occupations. Although the data on engineering and science students is a bit more limited, I assume in this book that the profiles of their personality traits and learning styles are similar to that of practicing engineers and scientists.

Because personality traits and learning styles have implications for learning and instruction, it behooves the science or engineering librarian to learn the typical personality traits and learning styles of their students. Before presenting findings about the typical personality traits and learning styles of scientists and engineers, I first highlight the learning styles and personality frameworks used in this book.

REFERENCES

Allen, J., & Robbins, S. B. (2008). Prediction of college major persistence based on vocational interests, academic preparation, and first-year academic performance. *Research in Higher Education, 49*(1), 62–79. http://dx.doi.org/10.1007/s11162-007-9064-5.

Baumeister, R. F., & Vohs, K. D. (2007). *Encyclopedia of social psychology.* Thousand Oaks, CA: Sage Publications.

Conn, S. R., & Rieke, M. L. (1994). *16PF fifth edition technical manual.* Champaign, IL: Institute for Personality and Ability Testing.

Gibson, L. W., Lounsbury, J. W., & Saudargas, R. A. (2004). An investigation of personality traits in relation to intention to withdraw from college. *Journal of College Student Development, 45*(5), 517–534. http://dx.doi.org/10.1353/csd.2004.0059.

Gottfredson, G. D., & Holland, J. L. (1996). *Dictionary of Holland occupational codes.* Odessa, FL: Psychological Assessment Resources Inc.

Haemmerlie, F. M., & Montgomery, R. L. (2012). Gender differences in the academic performance and retention of undergradute engineering majors. *College Student Journal, 46*(1), 40.

Holland, J. L. (1973). *Making vocational choices.* Englewood Cliffs, NJ: Prentice-Hall.

Holland, J. L. (1985). *Making vocational choices: A theory of vocational personalities and work environments.* Englewood Cliffs, NJ: Prentice Hall.

Holland, J. L. (1997). *Making vocational choices: A theory of vocational personalities and work environments.* Odessa, FL: Psychological Assessment Resources.

Kolb, D. A. (2015). *Experiential learning: Experience as the source of learning and development* (2nd ed.). Upper Saddle River, NJ: Pearson Education Ltd.

Kolb, A. Y., & Kolb, D. A. (2013). *The Kolb Learning Style Inventory 4.0: A comprehensive guide to the theory, psychometrics, research on validity and educational applications.* Experience Based Learning Systems, Inc.

Lerner, R. M., Easterbrooks, M. A., & Mistry, J. (Eds.), (2013). *Developmental psychology.* (2nd ed.) Hoboken, NJ: John Wiley & Sons, Inc.

Lounsbury, J. W., Loveland, J. M., Sundstrom, E. D., Gibson, L. W., Drost, A. W., & Hamrick, F. L. (2003). An investigation of personality traits in relation to career satisfaction. *Journal of Career Assessment, 11*(3), 287–307. http://dx.doi.org/10.1177/1069072703254501.

Lounsbury, J. W., Sundstrom, E., Loveland, J. M., & Gibson, L. W. (2003). Intelligence, "Big Five" personality traits, and work drive as predictors of course grade. *Personality and Individual Differences, 35*(6), 1231–1239. http://dx.doi.org/10.1016/S0191-8869(02)00330-6.

Moses, L., Hall, C., Wuensch, K., De Urquidi, K., Kauffmann, P., Swart, W., et al. (2011). Are math readiness and personality predictive of first-year retention in engineering? *The Journal of Psychology, 145*(3), 229–245. http://dx.doi.org/10.1080/00223980.2011.557749.

Rosati, P. (1993). Student retention from first-year engineering related to personality type. In: *Paper presented at the 23rd annual conference on frontiers in education: Engineering education: Renewing America's technology, November 6, 1993–November 9, 1993, Washington, DC.* http://dx.doi.org/10.1109/FIE.1993.405572.

Sullivan, L. E. (2009). *The Sage glossary of the social and behavioral sciences.* Thosand Oaks, CA: Sage.

Vedel, A. (2016). Big Five personality group differences across academic majors: A systematic review. *Personality and Individual Differences, 92*, 1–10. http://dx.doi.org/10.1016/j.paid.2015.12.011.

Walsh, W. B., Craik, K. H., & Price, R. H. (2000). *Person-environment psychology: New directions and perspectives.* Mahwah, NJ: Erlbaum.

CHAPTER 2

Learning Styles

2.1 DEFINITION OF LEARNING STYLES

Kolb (2015) viewed learning styles as "possibility-processing structures," or patterns of transaction between the individual and his or her environment.

> *The concept of possibility-processing structure gives central importance to the role of individual choice in decision making. The way we process the possibilities of each new emerging event determines the range of choices and decisions we see. The choices and decisions we make, to some extent, determine the events we live through, and these events influence our future choices.*

Thus, for Kolb, learning styles were not fixed "types," but contextually created self-programming causing people to emphasize elements of learning (Concrete Experience vs Abstract Conceptualization and Reflective Observation vs Active Experimentation).

Different learning styles theorists have viewed learning styles as having varying degrees of stability, with some being more trait-like than others. (Coffield, Moseley, Hall, & Ecclestone, 2004). Because learning styles are not construed as fixed traits in Kolb's definition, I view them as more descriptive than predictive. Kolb pointed out that the Learning Styles Instrument "was not intended to be a predictive psychological test like, IQ, GRE, or GMAT," but, rather, "a self-assessment exercise and a means for construct validation of experiential learning theory" (2015).

Learning styles in Kolb's theory are states rather than traits, and can change depending on an individual's experiences. Kolb describes the example of engineers who move into managerial positions and begin focusing more on Concrete Experience than they did in the past as they learn to deal with personnel matters in addition to abstract technical problems. Similarly, a science or engineering student might be attracted to certain styles of learning as a function of personality and experiences, but their learning styles could change.

Learning styles do have some degree of consistency in a discipline or profession as a whole; however, because specialties tend to accentuate valued styles of learning. As an engineering student learns to solve technical

Teaching to Individual Differences in Science and Engineering Librarianship
http://dx.doi.org/10.1016/B978-0-08-101881-1.00002-9

problems by applying abstract principles, he or she will become more proficient in the learning style corresponding to Abstract Conceptualization and
Active Experimentation in Kolb's framework.

2.2 WHY I CHOSE THE KOLB MODEL FOR THIS BOOK

Before explaining the specifics of the Kolb Learning Styles Model, I will
first address Coffield et al.'s (2004) criticisms of it and my reasons for choosing it. Coffield et al., in a highly influential systematic and critical review of
learning styles models and their instruments, weighed the evidence for and
against Kolb's model. Coffield et al. criticized the test re-test reliability and
validity of the learning styles instruments developed by Kolb before the date
of the Coffield et al. review (2004). They also criticized the validity of the
learning cycle model developed by Kolb.

Test re-test reliability has to do with the ability of test results to be re-
produced on later occasions of taking the test. Coffield et al. (2004) noted
that previous versions of the Learning Styles Inventory had low test re-
test reliability. A possible reason for this is that according to Kolb's formulation, learning styles are flexible across situations to some degree. The Kolb
Learning Styles Inventory 4.0 (Kolb & Kolb, 2013) does have acceptable internal consistency reliability; however, which means the items for each scale
measure the same construct represented by that scale. For example, the items
that measure Reflective Observation tend to be correlated with each other.

Coffield et al.'s criticism of the validity of Kolb's Learning Style Inventory
is concerned with the mixed and scanty evidence about matching students'
learning styles to instruction, which has a statistically significant effect on
learning. Kolb and Kolb (2013) present evidence; however, that learning
styles may affect performance on different kinds of assessment methods,
that diversity of learning styles may improve team performance, and that
learning styles may influence preference for teaching methods.

Coffield et al. also criticized Kolb's formulation of a four-part learning
cycle based on two dimensions (Abstract Conceptualization vs Concrete
Experience and Active Experimentation vs Reflective Observation). They
summarize evidence that the model may be statistically reducible to one
dimension. An implication of this finding is that an educator should consider whether both of the dimensions describe meaningful differences for
learning.

I believe that both of the dimensions that are the basis of the Kolb
model describe meaningful learning preference differences. For example, a

preference for Abstract Conceptualization versus Concrete Experience leads to quite different interests. The person who prefers Concrete Experience will enjoy learning in concrete situations involving people whereas the person preferring Abstract Conceptualization will prefer learning about general ideas and concepts. Similarly, the person who prefers Reflective Observation will be more interested in reflecting upon knowledge rather than applying it, which a person preferring Active Experimentation would want to do.

While Coffield et al. have brought plenty of evidence that early versions of Kolb's Learning Styles Inventory had psychometric problems, I do not believe they have debunked Kolb's theory, which has value for the instructor wishing to understand individual differences in learning preferences. If the Kolb learning styles theory prompts instructors to use a wide range of teaching styles and gives them a conceptual understanding of ways students differ, it at least does these two important things.

I also chose to use the Kolb model because the typical learning styles of people in different academic specializations tend to be what would be expected by Kolb's experiential learning theory. For example, the average learning style of engineers is abstract and active, which seems to align well with engineers' active application of abstract scientific and technical knowledge in their occupations. The average scores for other disciplines are also as would be expected by the types of knowledge studied by these disciplines. It also seems to me that the new version of the Kolb Learning Styles Inventory 4.0 may address psychometric problems in earlier versions of the Kolb instrument (A.Y. Kolb & Kolb, 2013).

2.3 THE KOLB LEARNING STYLES CYCLE

Kolb's learning style model is based on his theory of experiential learning, which states that ideas are "formed and re-formed from experience." Learning is a process based on the learner's experience, since new ideas are always modified by the experiences of the learner.

Kolb viewed learning as shaped by dialectical relationships between:
1. Concrete Experience and Abstract Conceptualization
2. Reflective Observation and Active Experimentation

He developed an idealized "learning cycle" modeling the process of learning. The cycle begins with Concrete Experience, proceeds to Reflective Observation, is followed by Abstract Conceptualization, and then is succeeded by Active Experimentation. As Kolb points out,

Our learning style may dictate where we begin a process of learning and/or the context may shape it. Learning usually does not happen in one big cycle but in numerous small cycles or partial cycles.

Cowan, an engineering educator, in his thorough discussion of the use of reflection in university learning, depicted alterations of the idealized learning cycle, showing, for example, the case when one phase might double back to the preceding phase (2006).

I view Kolb's model as important for explaining that learning at times can be concrete, abstract, reflective, or active. A full model of learning would need to acknowledge that all of these elements are important to the learning process. Concrete learning (Concrete Experience) might take place in a specific situation in a student's sensory awareness that serves as a stimulus for additional learning. Reflective Observation is the stage in which the student thinks about the situation using multiple perspectives. Abstract Conceptualization is the stage in which the student relates general, abstract principles to his or her observations. Active Experimentation is the phase in which the student applies these abstract concepts to test them out, which perhaps leads to solving a real-world problem.

Kolb (2015) initially posited that students used four learning styles corresponding to preferences for different parts of the learning cycle:

1. Accommodation, emphasizing Active Experimentation and Concrete Experience
2. Divergence, emphasizing Concrete Experience and Reflective Observation
3. Assimilation, emphasizing Reflective Observation and Abstract Conceptualization
4. Convergence, emphasizing Abstract Conceptualization and Active Experimentation

- Accommodators tend to be oriented towards "carrying out plans and tasks and getting involved in new experiences." Accommodators are adaptive to new experiences and sometimes take risks. They solve problems in an intuitive, trial-and-error manner and tend to get information from people, rather than theories.
- Divergers have great imaginative ability and are aware of meaning and values. "The primary adaptive ability of divergence is to view concrete situations from many perspectives and to organize many relationships into a meaningful 'gestalt.'" Divergers are people-focused and feeling-oriented.
- Assimilators are good at inductive reasoning and creating theoretical models, "in assimilating disparate observations into an integrated

explanation." They are focused on ideas and abstract concepts more than people and are concerned with theories being logical.

- Convergers are good at "problem solving, decision making, and the practical application of ideas." They tend to use hypothetical–deductive reasoning to solve problems. They control their emotions and would rather deal with technical problems and tasks than interpersonal or social matters.

In the latest revision of their learning styles instrument, the Kolb Learning Style Inventory 4.0 (2013), David and Alice Kolb expanded the learning style types to nine. The following table shows the styles, along with their positions on the Concrete Experience-Abstract Conceptualization and Reflective Observation-Active Experimentation dimensions.[5]

Type	CE	RO	AC	AE
Initiating	High	Low	Low	High

Strengths: Committing to objectives
Seeking new opportunities
Influencing and leading others
Weaknesses: Controlling the impulse to act
Listening to others views
Impatience

Experiencing	High	Balanced with AE	Low	Balanced with RO

Strengths: Building deep personal relationships
Strong intuition focused by reflection and action
Open to new experiences
Weaknesses: Understanding theory
Systematic planning
Evaluation

Imagining (Creating)	High	High	Low	Low

Strengths: Awareness of people's feelings and values
Listening with an open mind
Imagining the implications of ambiguous situations
Weaknesses: Decision-making
Taking leadership
Timely action

(Continued)

[5]Descriptions of the nine types are used with permission from Alice Y. Kolb (A.Y. Kolb & Kolb, 2013).

Type	CE	RO	AC	AE
Reflecting	Balanced with AC	High	Balanced with CE	Low

Strengths: Understanding others' point of view
Seeing "What's going on" in situations
Converting intuitions into explicit explanations
Gathering information
Weaknesses: Initiating action
Rumination
Speaking up in groups

Analyzing	Low	High	High	Low

Strengths: Organizing information
Being logical and rational
Building conceptual models
Weaknesses: Risk-taking
Socializing with others
Dealing with lack of structure

Thinking	Low	Balanced with AE	High	Balanced with RO

Strengths: Logical analysis
Rational decision-making
Analyzing quantitative data
Weaknesses: Working with people
Keeping an open mind about your ideas
"Lost in thought"

Deciding	Low	Low	High	High

Strengths: Problem-solving
Evaluating ideas and solutions
Setting goals
Making decisions
Weaknesses: Thinking "out of the box"
Sensitivity to people's feelings
Dealing with ambiguity

Acting	Balanced with AC	Low	Balanced with CE	High

Strengths: Combining technical knowledge and personal relationships
Focused on getting things done
Leading work teams
Weaknesses: Taking time to reflect
Solving the right problem
Gathering and analyzing information

Type	CE	RO	AC	AE
Balancing[a]	Balanced with RO, AC, and AE	Balanced with CE, AC, and AE	Balanced with CE, RO, and AE	Balanced with CE, RO, and AC

Strengths: Flexibility in moving around the learning cycle
Ability to work with diverse groups of people
Creative insights
Weaknesses: Indecisiveness
"Jack of all trades, master of none."
Sustained commitment

[a]According to Alice Y. Kolb (personal communication), there are two other profiles of Balancing learners besides the one where RO, AC, AE, and CE are approximately equal. Balancing learners may also have equally high AC and CE and equally low AE and RO. Alternatively, they may have equally high AE and RO and equally low CE and AC.

This expanded framework increases the granularity of Kolb's learning style theory, but past research works with the four learning styles.

2.4 INSTRUCTIONAL DESIGN EXAMPLES USING THE KOLB LEARNING STYLES FRAMEWORK

Kolb and Kolb (2013) point out several ways in which the use of Experiential Learning Theory can be useful in instruction:

> The ELT holistic approach proposes that learning interventions that foster all four learning modes result in more effective learning outcomes. The holistic approach engages all learners by appealing to their preferred style at some point in the learning process, thus providing a way for all learners to enter the cycle. Additionally, a holistic approach enhances the learner's flexibility in enacting different styles over time, as well as increasing learning comprehension and retention (p. 91).

In engineering education, experiential learning theory has been used in a variety of ways. I discuss here applications of Kolb's learning styles/learning cycle to teamwork, design education, and specific engineering topics.

2.4.1 Teamwork

Sharp (1998, 2001) used Kolb learning styles theory to teach teamwork and communication skills to engineering students. She taught the students the basics of the theory and asked them to reflect on their own learning style and how they were affected by people with different learning styles in team communication. In a technical communication class, Sharp had students prepare presentations that were designed to contain elements appealing to all four learning styles. In a combined chemical engineering lab/technical communication class, Sharp had students reflect on strengths, weaknesses, and possible sources of conflict in teams composed of individuals with opposite learning style types. The students also kept teamwork notebooks discussing the impact of learning styles on interactions between team members in lab activities.

Sharp's assignments thus encouraged students to develop metacognitive skills drawing upon learning styles theory. These skills would enable students to apply their knowledge of learning styles theory in other teamwork communication settings. Thinking about learning styles evidently gave them strategies for adapting communication and understanding interactions with other people. Another possible application of Kolb's learning style theory is forming teams based on learning styles. Sharp makes the point that this would have been difficult to do in her classes because often there were very few Divergers and Accommodators (2001).

Lau, Beckman, and Agogino (2012) evaluated team composition in a graduate design class, finding that teams with only one Converger enjoyed working together more than those with two or more Convergers. There were several other significant findings, as well, tending to indicate that teams with one Converger and that were gender-diverse did the best. Although Convergers were the predominant learning style type in the class, it seems that encouraging diversity in team composition led to better outcomes than grouping the Convergers together in teams. Lau et al. hypothesized that these results might be due to Convergers' internal focus, stating, "Perhaps an entire team of persistent thinkers translates to little or no reflective dialogue within the team, and limited or slower success in teamwork" (p. 297).

2.4.2 Design Courses and Internships

Experiential learning theory would seem to be very useful for experience-based design courses, internships, and problem-based learning. Wegner, Turcic, and Hohner (2015) pointed out that the Multidisciplinary Design Program at the University of Michigan had the following goals:

"to produce students (1) possessing deep technical skills and the ability to be systems thinkers; (2) capable and skilled in bringing creativity and innovation to design and problem-solving; (3) who are independent learners, able to reinvest themselves throughout their careers; and (4) who are effective communicators and team players in their professional and personal lives." Wegner et al. used a reflective learning approach incorporating the Kolb learning framework to foster these goals in a leadership class within the design program.

Just as Sharp's technical communication classes used Kolb learning styles theory to instill soft skills in students, design courses have also used this content to prompt students to reflect on their personal strengths and weaknesses, and to appreciate the diversity of other individuals. For example, Schmidt et al. (2003) incorporated Kolb Learning Styles and other self-discovery instruments into the project team curriculum at the University of Maryland and partner schools and had students incorporate these in learning about personal and interpersonal domains.

Another interesting synergy between Kolb learning styles/learning cycle theory and design classes is the fact that there are similarities between the learning cycle and elements of the design process. Owen, in a general model of the design process (1998), distinguishes between Analytic and Synthetic design (which seems to correspond to Kolb's reflective and active dimensions), and Symbolic and Real design (which seems to correspond to Kolb's abstract and concrete dimensions). Research degrees in design fall into the Analytic category, whereas professional degrees fall into the Synthetic category. Design planning is an example of Symbolic design, and human-centered design ("concerned with the specifics of form and function") is an example of Real Design.

In the field of architectural design, Demirbas and Demirkan showed an empirical relationship between learning styles and the stages of the architectural design process (2003). Assimilators, Convergers, and Accommodators did better at different parts of a design course. While it may not be valid to generalize findings from architectural design to engineering design, it is notable that a few engineering educators have explored connections between the Kolb learning cycle and design. For example, Ogot and Okudan (2007) compare the stages of TRIZ (theory of inventive problem solving) with the Kolb model. TRIZ is a systematic concept generation process.

The first stage of TRIZ, "Decompose and understand the problem" corresponds loosely to Concrete Experience and Reflective Observation (Divergers). The second stage, "Determine general design parameters. Define technical contradiction. From tables obtain suggested design principles" corresponds to Abstract Conceptualization and Reflective Observation (Assimilators). The third stage, "Study examples of the application of suggested design principles. Determine how principles applied" loosely corresponds to Abstract Conceptualization and Active Experimentation (Convergers). The fourth stage, "Apply principles to current problem. Explore different variations and combinations" corresponds to Concrete Experience and Active Experimentation (Accommodators).

Ogot and Okudan state, "The use of TRIZ, therefore, in conjunction with traditional ideation methods would meet (at one point in the cycle) the learning style preferences of all engineering students …" (p. 574). Other models of the engineering design process seem to have similarities to the Kolb learning cycle, as well. For example, Radcliffe's elemental engineering design activities include seven steps, the middle stages of which appear to correspond to the learning cycle (2014):

1. *Organize Your Team*—Develop Knowledge Management Strategy
2. ***Clarify the Task***—Establish the Project Context (Concrete Experience, Reflective Observation)
3. ***Synthesize Possibilities***—Investigate Prior Art (Abstract Conceptualization, Reflective Observation)
4. ***Select Solution***—Assess Technologies and Methods (Abstract Conceptualization, Active Experimentation)
5. ***Refine Solution***—Integrate Technical Details (Concrete Experience, Active Experimentation)
6. *Communicate Effectively With All Stakeholders*—Distill Project Knowledge
7. *Improve Design Work Processes*

Similarities can be seen between steps 2–5 of Radcliffe's model of the design process and Kolb's learning cycle.

1. Divergers (Concrete Experience and Reflective Observation) like to listen, interact, and brainstorm.
   Clarifying the Project Task would seem to fall into this quadrant since it involves listening to the customer about requirements for the design.
2. Assimilators (Reflective Observation and Abstract Conceptualization) like to analyze, classify, form theories, and observe.
   Synthesizing Possibilities would seem to fall into this quadrant since it involves investigating the current state of knowledge and coming up with a proposed technical solution.
3. Convergers (Abstract Conceptualization and Active Experimentation) apply learning and are good at experimenting and improving things.
   Selecting a Solution would seem to belong to this quadrant since it involves testing proposed solutions.
4. Accommodators (Active Experimentation and Concrete Experience) like to create, take risks, and adapt.
   Refining the Solution would appear to dovetail with this quadrant since it involves visualization of the design model, fleshing out the manufacturing details, and risk and opportunity analysis.

A possible implication of the similarity between the Kolb model and the design process is that instructional strategies that take into account all the stages of the learning cycle may be especially beneficial for design classes. Engineering educators may even already instruct to the stages of the learning cycle without being aware of it, simply because the design process is similar.

2.4.3 Specific Engineering Topics

Ammerman, Sen, and Streveler (2005) applied the Kolb learning styles model to a class on solving Grid power flow problems. Students were first encouraged to reflect on why the power flow problem was significant (Concrete Experience and Reflective Observation). Then they learned about formulas for solving power flow problems (Abstract Conceptualization and Reflective Observation). Then they used a computer simulation program to solve a power flow problem (Active Experimentation and Abstract Conceptualization). Last, they were given open-ended design problems to solve with the simulation program (Concrete Experience and Abstract Experimentation). When students were asked what helped them learn in the course, responses were generally positive. Interestingly, the two comments that Ammerman et al. include indicate that students were responding to different parts of the learning cycle. One student liked seeing the mathematics behind solving power flow problems and then using a computer simulation program to solve this sort of problem. Another wanted more open-ended design problems. Based on these comments, it seems that it was beneficial to use a variety of teaching methods to appeal to different kinds of learners.

David, Wyrick, and Hilsen (2002) applied the Kolb learning cycle to industrial engineering classes. Finding over a period of 10 years that upper level industrial engineering students were predominantly Convergers (favoring Active Experimentation and Abstract Conceptualization), the authors tried to make the students more well-rounded by incorporating other stages of the learning cycle in the instruction. To give one example, the instructors asked students to confer with stakeholders about a homecoming bonfire site selection in one class. Course evaluations for this class and others where the instructors tried to incorporate experiential learning were poor, but the instructors felt that students had learned a great deal. In my opinion, a possible explanation for the poor course evaluations is that students were stretched to use learning styles they did not prefer, causing them to feel that they were not learning much.

Hein and Budny (1999) discussed applying the Kolb learning cycle to a calculus class for at-risk freshmen engineering students. One-on-one counseling about difficulties in solving calculus problems was supposed to appeal to Divergers. Organized lectures were supposed to appeal to Assimilators. The chance to re-do assignments that received a grade of less than B was supposed to appeal to Convergers. The opportunity for self-learning in small groups with a tutor was supposed to appeal to Accommodators. Unfortunately, Hein and Budny did not formally assess the effectiveness of these approaches, but they stated that the attention given to learner diversity contributed to the success of their teaching and learning strategies.

Wartman (2006) applied the Kolb learning cycle to teaching geotechnical physical modeling. Photographs of shallow foundations and a physical model demonstration gave students a Concrete Experience activity. Next students engaged in Reflective Observation by viewing a video of the experiment and making measurements and observations. A classroom lecture on bearing capacity engaged students in Abstract Conceptualization. Finally, a classroom problem-solving activity and homework assignment stimulated students to engage in Active Experimentation. Analysis of a second physical model allowed students to apply the theoretical and experiential knowledge they had gained, bringing the students back to Concrete Experience in the learning cycle. Wartman stated that an effect of the application of the learning cycle was that it prevented the "pendulum style" of teaching in which teaching alternates between lecture and homework.

Plett and Ciletti (2005) used the Kolb learning cycle in an introduction to robotics course. They operationalized the learning cycle using the 4MAT model (McCarthy & McCarthy, 2006), which has been used by many engineering educators. The 4MAT model links different kinds of instructional activities with the four Kolb learning styles in quadrants. Plett and Ciletti state:

Our approach to Introduction to Robotics addresses all four quadrants of the 4MAT® method illustrated by Figure 1. Motivational examples, stories, and interactive discussions (Quadrant 1) serve to stimulate interest in robotics; our formal lectures, reading assignments, and demonstrations (Quadrant 2) provide a base of knowledge to support the laboratory work in Quadrant 3, where a guided series of progressively more difficult robot projects unfolds over eight weeks. Quizzes are administered to encourage study and evaluate progress. The first three quadrants of the 4MAT® cycle set the stage for the last, a seven-week self-guided experience in which our students engage in an open-ended design project requiring them to develop a conceptual approach and design a robot to compete against other robots while adhering to constraints that limit the resources that can be used. Thus this course takes our students through a complete cycle of the 4MAT® experience.

As can be seen from the preceding examples, the Kolb learning styles framework has been of interest to engineering educators in a variety of disciplines. The examples cited here do not formally assess the efficacy of incorporating a diverse set of learning activities in instruction, nor do they match particular activities to students with different learning styles. Instead, the instructors attempt to create well-rounded courses that could appeal to a variety of learning preferences.

2.5 CONCLUSION

The Kolb Learning Styles model allows the instructor to conceptualize ways learners may differ in respect to their preferences for abstract, concrete, active, and reflective learning. Because Kolb's framework shows that there are empirical differences in respect to learning styles among members of disciplines, it can be used to describe differences between librarians, engineers, scientists, or other groups. In addition, teaching to different parts of the learning cycle may make students more well-rounded, as well as engage different kinds of learners.

REFERENCES

Ammerman, R. F., Sen, P. K., & Streveler, R. A. (2005). Work in progress: The Kolb learning model applied to an advanced energy systems laboratory. In *Paper presented at the frontiers in education conference, Indianapolis, IN*.

Coffield, F., Moseley, D., Hall, E., & Ecclestone, K. (2004). Learning styles and pedagogy in post 16 learning: A systematic and critical review. London: The Learning and Skills Research Centre.

Cowan, J. (2006). On becoming an innovative university teacher: Reflection in action (2nd ed.). New York, NY: Society for Research into Higher education & Open University Press.

David, A., Wyrick, P., & Hilsen, L. (2002). Using Kolb's cycle to round out learning. In *Paper presented at the proceedings of the 2002 American Society for Engineering Education annual conference & exposition*.

Demirbas, O., & Demirkan, H. (2003). Focus on architectural design process through learning styles. *Design Studies, 24*(5), 437–456. http://dx.doi.org/10.1016/S0142-694X(03)00013-9.

Hein, T. L., & Budny, D. D. (1999). Teaching to students' learning styles: Approaches that work. In *Paper presented at the frontiers in education conference, 1999. FIE'99. 29th annual*.

Kolb, D. A. (2015). Experiential learning: Experience as the source of learning and development (2nd ed.). Upper Saddle River, NJ: Pearson Education Ltd.

Kolb, A. Y., & Kolb, D. A. (2013). The Kolb Learning Style Inventory 4.0: A comprehensive guide to the theory, psychometrics, research on validity and educational applications. Experience Based Learning Systems, Inc.

Lau, K., Beckman, S. L., & Agogino, A. M. (2012). Diversity in design teams: An investigation of learning styles and their impact on team performance and innovation. *International Journal of Engineering Education, 28*(2), 293–301.

McCarthy, B., & McCarthy, D. (2006). Teaching around the 4MAT® cycle: Designing instruction for diverse learners with diverse learning styles. Thousand Oaks, CA: Corwin Press.

Ogot, M., & Okudan, G. E. (2007). Systematic creativity methods in engineering education: A learning styles perspective. *International Journal of Engineering Education, 22*(3), 566.

Owen, C. L. (1998). Design research: Building the knowledge base. *Design Studies, 19*(1), 9–20. http://dx.doi.org/10.1016/S0142-694X(97)00030-6.

Plett, G. L., & Ciletti, M. D. (2005). Piloting a balanced curriculum in electrical engineering—Introduction to robotics. In *Paper presented at the proceedings of the 2005 American Society of Engineering Education annual conference and exposition, Portland, OR.*

Radcliffe, D. F. (2014). Information-rich engineering design. In M. Fosmire & D. F. Radcliffe (Eds.), *Integrating information into the engineering design process* (pp. 45–57). West LaFayette, IN: Purdue University Press.

Schmidt, L., Schmidt, J., Colbeck, C., Bigio, D., Smith, P., & Harper, L. (2003). Engineering students and training in teamwork: How effective? In *Paper presented at the 2003 ASEE annual conference and exposition: Staying in tune with engineering education, June 22, 2003–June 25, 2003, Nashville, TN, United States.*

Sharp, J. E. (1998). Learning styles and technical communication: Improving communication and teamwork skills. In *Paper presented at the proceedings of the 1998 28th annual frontiers in education conference, Fie. part 3 (of 3), November 4, 1998–November 7, 1998, Tempe, AZ, United States.*

Sharp, J. E. (2001). Teaching teamwork communication with Kolb learning style theory. In *Paper presented at the 31st annual frontiers in education conference—Impact on engineering and science education, October 10, 2001–October 13, 2001, Reno, NV, United States.*

Wartman, J. (2006). Geotechnical physical modeling for education: Learning theory approach. *Journal of Professional Issues in Engineering Education and Practice, 132*(4), 288–296. http://dx.doi.org/10.1061/(ASCE)1052-3928(2006)132:4(288).

Wegner, J., Turcic, S. M., & Hohner, G. (2015). Learning from experiences: Examining self-reflection in engineering de-sign courses. In *Paper presented at the 122nd ASEE annual conference & exposition, Seattle, WA.*

CHAPTER 3

Personality Frameworks

3.1 DEFINITION OF PERSONALITY

Entwistle cites Allport's definition of personality as "the dynamic organization within the individual of those psychophysical systems that determine his characteristic behavior and thought" (2013). Following this definition, Entwistle states that personality can change with experience; it depends on both psychological and physical attributes; and it determines characteristic thought and behavior. In addition, he states, "... it hints at physiological systems common to everyone, yet points to the ultimate uniqueness of the individual." If one accepts Entwistle's definition, one would agree that personality has some degree of malleability while also producing characteristic traits in an individual.

3.2 RELATIONSHIPS BETWEEN PERSONALITY AND TEACHING AND LEARNING

Intersections between personality, teaching, and learning depend on both the instructor's personality and the student's personality. In the case of the instructor, his or her personality traits may influence classroom behavior and the course evaluations he or she receives. In the case of students, their personality traits can affect their engagement, participation, and self-regulation.

3.2.1 Instructor Classroom Behavior

The personality traits of instructors have long been known to influence their classroom behavior. For example, Erdle, Murray, and Rushton (1985) found that instructors who displayed the following traits exhibited "charismatic" classroom behaviors: dominant, show leadership, enduring, intellectually-curious, attention-seeking, supporting, fun-loving, objective, aesthetically

Teaching to Individual Differences in Science and
Engineering Librarianship
http://dx.doi.org/10.1016/B978-0-08-101881-1.00003-0

sensitive, sociable, Extraverted, changeable, liberal, and approval-seeking. On the other hand, the trait of being authoritarian was negatively associated with charismatic classroom behavior, and harm avoidance, defensiveness, and anxiety approached having statistically significant negative correlations with charismatic behaviors. A number of other personality traits seem to be important for effective teaching. For example, Cornelius–White examined the effect of person-centered teacher variables on student outcomes in a metaanalysis of previous studies (2007).[6] Teacher empathy and warmth had significant correlations with student outcomes. Both empathy and warmth are related to personality, as can be seen by descriptions of 16PF factors A (Warmth) and I (Sensitivity).[7] Similarly, teacher enthusiasm was a strong predictor of student intrinsic motivation and vitality in one study (B.C. Patrick, Hisley, & Kempler, 2000). Enthusiasm is related to descriptions of the 16PF Factor F (Liveliness).

3.2.2 Course Evaluations

There is a large body of literature associated with the correlations between teacher personality traits and ratings or evaluations from students. To summarize a few of the findings, instructors scoring higher on the Big Five trait, Agreeableness, received higher course evaluations than less Agreeable ones at one university (Kneipp, Kelly, Biscoe, & Richard, 2010). Clayson and Sheffet also found that course evaluations were positively correlated with students' ratings of instructors' personality traits of Agreeableness, Creativity, Conscientiousness, Stability, and Extraversion across nine undergraduate business classes (2006). Similarly, C.L. Patrick found that students in five education classes who thought instructors were more Extraverted, open, agreeable, and conscientious gave the instructors higher course evaluation ratings (2011).

3.2.3 Student Engagement

Douglas, Bore, and Munro (2016) defined work engagement in this way:

Work engagement is defined by Schaufeli, Salanova, et al. (2002) as a "… positive, fulfilling, work-related state of mind" (p. 74). Work engagement consists of three affective-cognitive states. Vigor is characterized by high levels of mental resilience

---

[6]Meta-analyses use statistical techniques to summarize the overall findings of studies measuring the same variables.
[7]Later in this chapter I define the factors in more detail.

while working, a willingness to invest effort in work, and persistence with work activities. Dedication refers to a sense of enthusiasm, pride, and challenge towards work. Absorption refers to being concentrated and engrossed in work.

Douglas et al. administered the Big Five Aspect Scales and the Utrecht Work Engagement Survey, as well as a Time Management Behaviour Scale to 281 students. There were several significant relationships between students' engagement and personality.

Table 3.1 explains the Big Five personality aspects, as well as the Big Five personality facets, because some of the studies cited in this book refer to the aspects or the facets. Basically aspects are important subelements of the Big Five personality traits that can be studied separately. For example, Volatility and Withdrawal are the two aspects of Neuroticism (Douglas et al., 2016). Facets are the several narrower traits under the Big Five traits. For example, Fantasy is a facet of Openness to Experience (Costa & McCrae, 1992). Each of the larger Big Five traits has two poles: for example, low scorers on Extraversion are more introverted, whereas high scorers are more Extraverted.

Table 3.1 Big Five personality traits, aspects, and facets

Big Five trait	Aspects	Facets
Openness to Experience-high scorers are curious, imaginative, innovative, and have wide interests	Openness-high scorers enjoy beauty, are creative, and tend to get lost in thought Intellect-high scorers like solving challenging problems and enjoy complexity	Ideas (having curiosity) Fantasy (being imaginative) Aesthetics (having artistic interests) Actions (having wide interests) Feelings (excitableness) Values (being unconventional)
Extraversion-high scorers are energetic, talkative, sociable, active, and assertive	Assertiveness-high scorers take charge and are quick to act Enthusiasm-high scorers like to have fun with other people	Gregariousness (sociability) Assertiveness (forcefulness) Activity (having energy) Excitement-seeking (adventurousness) Positive emotions (enthusiasm) Warmth (outgoingness)

(Continued)

Table 3.1 · Big Five personality traits, aspects, and facets—cont'd

Big Five trait	Aspects	Facets
Agreeableness-high scorers are kind, appreciative of others, and altruistic	Politeness-high scorers are considerate and avoid conflict with others Compassion-high scorers are interested in others and concerned about their well-being	Trust (quick to forgive) Straightforwardness (not demanding of others) Altruism (welcoming of others) Compliance (low in stubbornness) Modesty (humble, does not brag) Tender-mindedness (is sympathetic to others)
Conscientiousness-high scorers are organized, reliable, make plans, and are thorough	Industriousness-high scorers get to work quickly and stay focused Orderliness-high scorers like to follow a routine, pay attention to details and are tidy	Competence (efficiency) Order (being organized) Dutifulness (follows rules) Achievement striving (work hard) Self-discipline (doesn't waste time; industrious) Deliberation (don't rush into things)
Neuroticism-high scorers worry a lot, are self-pitying, touchy, and emotionally unstable. (Emotional Stability is the name for this trait at the opposite pole.)	Volatility-high scorers have difficulty controlling their emotions Withdrawal-high scorers worry a lot and get discouraged and overwhelmed	Anxiety (worries a lot) Angry hostility (irritability) Depression (feels blue and dissatisfied with self) Self-consciousness (is shy and gets embarrassed easily) Impulsiveness (has trouble resisting impulses such as temptations) Vulnerability (panics easily)

Sources: Douglas, H. E., Bore, M., & Munro, D. (2016). Coping with university education: The relationships of time management behaviour and work engagement with the five factor model aspects. *Learning and Individual Differences, 45*, 268–274. doi:10.1016/j.lindif.2015.12.004 (columns one and two); and Costa, P. T., & McCrae, R. R. (1992). *NEO Personality Inventory-Revised (NEO-PI-R)*. Odessa, FL: Psychological Assessment Resources (column 3).

Douglas et al. (2016) found that students who had greater Openness and Intellect, as well as greater Industriousness, scored higher on work engagement than students with lower values on these traits. Some work engagement subscales, such as vigor and absorption were negatively correlated with aspects of Neuroticism. Assertiveness and Compassion had positive correlations with some of the subscales of work engagement.

Consistent with these findings, Chamorro-Premuzic and Furnham (2009) found that Openness to experience was positively correlated with a deep learning approach and negatively with surface and achieving approaches. Deep learners have intrinsic interest in a topic and wish to develop competence in academic subjects. Surface learners want to meet requirements minimally, and achievement/strategic learners are competitive and wish to achieve the highest grade regardless of interest.

3.2.4 Student Participation

Personality traits are also associated with students' class participation. Caspi, Chajut, Saporta, and Beyth-Marom (2006) found in a study of a distance learning program that also had classroom meetings, that students who participated in a classroom environment were more Extraverted, Open to Experience, and emotionally stable than students who did not participate in class. Furnham and Medhurst (1995) found that Extraverted students participated more often in a psychology class academic seminar than more Introverted students (as measured by the 16PF).

3.2.5 Student Self-Regulation

Psychology students who were orderly and industrious (aspects of Conscientiousness) had better time management practices than students who scored lower on these traits (Douglas et al., 2016). Conscientiousness is associated with focusing on work and being planful and organized, so it is not surprising that more conscientious students would do better at managing their time.

3.3 THE 16PF AND BIG FIVE/NARROW PERSONALITY FRAMEWORKS

The two personality frameworks used in this book are the 16PF, originally developed by Cattell (Conn & Rieke, 1994), and the Big Five/Narrow Traits Personal Style Inventory developed by Lounsbury and Gibson (2006). Both of these inventories of personality traits were developed in the field of academic psychology, and they exhibit acceptable psychometric properties such as validity and reliability.[8]

---

[8]Validity refers to whether a test measures what it purports to measure. Reliability has to do with the accuracy of the test (Coaley, 2014). Both are used to evaluate whether a test is "good."

The instruments have somewhat different origins. The 16PF was developed over many years and editions through a statistical technique, factor analysis, that was used to discover the underlying dimensions of personality. Raymond Cattell factor analyzed a variety of data, such as linguistic descriptors of personal characteristics in the dictionary, peer ratings, self-reports, and behavioral observations (Cattell & Schuerger, 2003). He condensed all this data to 16 personality factors and five larger global factors.

Lounsbury and Gibson's Personal Style Inventory is an instrument that includes items measuring personality constructs known to be of importance in the psychological literature. These include the "Big Five" personality traits (Openness, Conscientiousness, Extraversion, Agreeableness, and Neuroticism/Emotional Stability) and several "narrow traits" known to be useful in predicting work–related and academic behavior (2006). The Big Five traits, which are similar to Cattell's composite factors, were also extensively studied by Costa and McCrae (1992), as well as others. They are accepted as basic personality traits that influence many kinds of behavior. Costa and McCrae, in their NEO instrument, also developed facets of the Big Five traits to give them greater specificity.

Both the 16PF and the Personal Style Inventory can be used to describe traits of groups or individuals. The 16PF was designed to incorporate all the basic personality factors that could be discovered by factor analysis and thus specifies a broad range of essential personality traits. The Personal Style Inventory contains the "Big Five" traits, which are considered basic personality traits, as well as several "narrow traits," such as Work Drive, Optimism, and Visionary Work Style, which supplement the Big Five in describing occupational and academic behavior.

The next sections of this chapter will define the traits in each of these personality frameworks, also providing examples of characteristics one might expect individuals to exhibit with low or high values.

3.3.1 The 16PF

The first factor (A) is Warmth. According to Cattell and Schuerger (2003), low scorers on Warmth tend to be reserved, formal, and unemotional, whereas high scorers are caring, empathetic, softhearted, and expressive. Low scorers tend to prefer working with things or ideas, rather than people, whereas the opposite is true for high scorers. Warmth correlates positively with the Big Five facets Warmth, Gregariousness, Positive Emotions, and Altruism (Conn & Rieke, 1994).

Low scorers on Warmth are objective and critical; very low scorers may avoid closeness with others. Walter points out that people scoring high in Warmth often prefer jobs where they have a lot of interpersonal contacts (2008). One might hypothesize based on this description that instructors high in Warmth would have an easier time teaching groups than those low in Warmth. Also one might guess that low scorers in Warmth would not enjoy group learning activities.

The second factor (B) is Reasoning. Low scorers have low abstract reasoning ability and perform less well in academic settings than high scorers, who are better at grasping abstract material (Cattell & Schuerger, 2003). Reasoning scores are based on 15 verbal, numerical, and logical reasoning questions, so may not be as reflective of general intelligence than a longer intelligence test.

Scientists and engineers have among the highest scores on Reasoning (Cattell & Schuerger, 2003). Low scorers include cooks, laborers, and members of other occupations that do not require a great deal of academic training. One would expect high scorers on Reasoning to appreciate challenging academic tasks and to "glaze over" if instruction is too easy. Lower scorers would be expected to have a difficult time grasping concepts that might not challenge their higher scoring peers and/or instructors.

The third factor is Emotional Stability (C). According to Cattell and Schuerger (2003), low scorers are reactive, emotional, and have a hard time dealing with stress. High scorers are resilient, calm, and deal well with stress. Emotional Stability is negatively correlated with the Big Five facets, Anxiety, Angry Hostility, Depression, Self-Consciousness, and Vulnerability (Conn & Rieke, 1994).

According to Cattell and Schuerger (2003), high scorers are drawn to occupations such as business, emergency services, and counseling. Low scorers may be drawn to less stressful jobs. Also, those with artistic temperaments may be low scorers (e.g., poets, designers, and musicians).

The fourth factor is Dominance (E). Low scorers are deferential, humble, diplomatic, and accommodating. High scorers are dominant, competitive, outspoken, and bossy. High scorers tend to have leadership qualities and are good at getting things done. Introverted dominant people may express their Dominance in nonsocial areas "such as by conquering new Intellectual frontiers or by 'sinking their teeth into' some problem" (Cattell & Schuerger, 2003). Dominance is negatively correlated with the Big Five NEO-PI-R facets, Self-Consciousness, Compliance, and Modesty (Conn & Rieke, 1994).

The fifth 16PF factor is Liveliness (F). Low scorers are serious and calculated in contrast to high scorers who are enthusiastic, spontaneous, and attention-seeking (Walter, 2008). Low Liveliness positively correlates with the Big Five NEO-PI-R facets, Warmth, Gregariousness, Excitement-Seeking, and Positive Emotions (Conn & Rieke, 1994). High scorers may be good at brainstorming and are stimulating in social interactions, and they may get bored easily. Low scorers on Liveliness have good powers of concentration and are reliable and dependable. They tend to be methodical and may lack a sense of humor (Cattell & Schuerger, 2003).

One would expect students with low Liveliness to be serious about their work and perhaps rather unresponsive in social interactions. Students with high Liveliness might get bored if instruction is not entertaining.

The sixth 16PF factor is Rule-Consciousness (G). Low scorers on Rule-Consciousness tend to be nonconforming and disregard rules. They are flexible and value autonomy. High scorers conform to group standards, value principles, and may be inflexible (Walter, 2008). Rule-Consciousness correlates positively with the Big Five facets Dutifulness, Achievement Striving, and Deliberation (Conn & Rieke, 1994). As Cattell and Schuerger (2003) point out, "This trait is adaptive in work that permits flexibility of approach and requires only minimal attention to fixed ways of doing things. For example, low scores are found among, artists, university professors, and psychotherapists."

Low scoring students may receive poor grades in high school or college. High scorers do well in structured occupational settings (Cattell & Schuerger, 2003). One would expect this to be the case in instructional settings as well. Highly Rule-Conscious students might prefer that instructors set clear rules and guidelines for behavior and assignments. Occupations that require creativity, such as scientists, tend to attract individuals with lower Rule-Consciousness, with physicists being the occupational group with the lowest scores (Cattell & Schuerger, 2003).

The seventh 16PF factor is Social Boldness (H). Low scorers are shy, socially conscious, and timid; high scorers are socially confident and bold in social interactions (Walter, 2008). Social Boldness correlates positively with the Big Five facets, Gregariousness, and Assertiveness (Conn & Rieke, 1994). High scorers may be found in high-stress and social occupations. Low scorers may be found in occupations involving less social contact and low stress (Cattell & Schuerger, 2003).

One would expect students with low Social Boldness to dislike interacting with people they do not know. Teachers with low Social Boldness might dislike teaching groups where they do not know the students, too.

The eighth factor is Sensitivity (I). Low scorers are objective, utilitarian, focused on getting things done, interested in how things work, and unsentimental. High scorers are sensitive, empathetic, subjective, and interested in aesthetics. They may base decisions on personal taste (Walter, 2008). As Cattell and Schuerger (2003) point out, low scorers may enjoy math more than English, may enjoy building things over reading, and may like mechanical things and inventions. Low scorers, in contrast to high scorers, may also be unable to tell what they or others are feeling.

High scorers on Sensitivity may be attracted to artistic or helping occupations. Low scorers may be found in technical occupations, such as engineering, among others (Cattell & Schuerger, 2003). Sensitivity is positively correlated with the NEO-PI-R facet, Aesthetics (Conn & Rieke, 1994).

The ninth factor is Vigilance (L). Low scorers are trusting, forgiving, and expect good intentions from others. High scorers are suspicious, untrusting of others, and may experience themselves as being separate from other people (Walter, 2008). High scorers are often good at detecting errors, and low scorers may be good team players (Cattell & Schuerger, 2003). Vigilance is correlated positively with the Big Five NEO-PI-R facets, Anxiety, Angry Hostility, and Depression and negatively with Trust (Conn & Rieke, 1994). One might expect high scoring students to be critical and suspicious of teachers' motives. Low scorers might be more accepting of teachers.

The tenth 16PF factor is Abstractedness (M). Low scorers are grounded, down to earth, concrete, and literal. High scorers are idea-oriented, self-absorbed, and sometimes absentminded (Walter, 2008). Low scorers may have good memories and be practical in emergencies, but may not be introspective or enjoy thinking about complex ideas (Cattell & Schuerger, 2003). Abstractedness correlates positively with the Big Five NEO-PI-R facet, Fantasy (Conn & Rieke, 1994). As Cattell and Schuerger (2003) point out, "Low scorers are not suited to occupations that require abstract, innovative thinking." High scorers are found in many artistic and scientific occupations, which require creativity.

The eleventh factor is Privateness (N). Low scorers are forthright, self-disclosing, and genuine. High scorers are guarded, private, and may be hard to get to know (Walter, 2008). High scorers might not like being asked personal questions and might be good social observers. Low scorers would most likely be socially expressive and straightforward. High scorers tend to be attracted to occupations that are relatively formal or that require diplomacy, such as counseling (Cattell & Schuerger, 2003).

Privateness correlates negatively with the Big Five facets, Warmth, Gregariousness, and Trust (Conn & Rieke, 1994).

The twelfth factor is Apprehension (O). Apprehension correlates positively with the Big Five facets, Anxiety, Angry Hostility, Depression, Self-Consciousness, and Vulnerability (Conn & Rieke, 1994). Low scorers tend to be self-assured, secure, and self-satisfied. High scorers are worried, insecure, and self-critical (Walter, 2008). High scorers may think about the consequences of their actions and have a strong sense of responsibility. Low scorers may be insensitive to others' feelings of anxiety or uncertainty (Cattell & Schuerger, 2003). One would expect low scoring students to be insensitive to feedback or evaluation, and high scorers to be anxious learners (or instructors).

The thirteenth factor is Openness to Change (Q1). Individuals who score low on Openness to Change are traditional and resist change. High scorers are open to change, experimenting, and enjoy variety (Walter, 2008). As Cattell and Schuerger (2003) note, "High scorers like to think freely and openly about things, without barriers or restrictions to logical thought. Thus, they tend to view things in new ways and to apply ideas from one field to another in creative ways. They enjoy experimenting with different solutions to problems rather than complacently accepting the tried-and-true solutions."

Openness to Change correlates positively with the Big Five facets, Aesthetics, Actions, and Ideas (Conn & Rieke, 1994). Occupations that attract individuals with high levels of Openness to Change include the arts, science, and engineering, all of which involve creative thinking (Cattell & Schuerger, 2003). Low-scoring occupations include clerical jobs, jobs that protect the *status quo*, such as police officers and firefighters, and realistic jobs such as mechanics.

The fourteenth factor is Self-Reliance (Q2). Low scorers are group-oriented team players that like to consult with others (Cattell & Schuerger, 2003). High scorers are self-sufficient, prefer their own ideas and opinions, and value autonomy. Self-Reliance correlates negatively with the Big Five facets Warmth, Gregariousness, Positive Emotions, and Trust (Conn & Rieke, 1994).

Highly Self-Reliant individuals tend to spend time alone and enjoy making decisions on their own, which can sometimes be an advantage. On the other hand, they may not enjoy collaboration. Low scorers may function well in groups, but sometimes have too strong a need to belong. They often choose occupations that require teamwork, such as nursing or social work. High scorers may be found in the arts, science, and computer science (Cattell & Schuerger, 2003).

The fifteenth factor is Perfectionism (Q3). Low scorers like unstructured, unpredictable situations, and are flexible. High scorers tend to be organized, planful, have good self-control, and want to do things right (Walter, 2008). Very high scorers may lack flexibility and creativity (Cattell & Schuerger, 2003). Low scorers may be casual and spontaneous and not set many goals. Perfectionism is positively correlated with the NEO-PI-R facets, Competence, Order, Dutifulness, Self-Discipline, and Deliberation (Conn & Rieke, 1994).

Occupations whose members often have high levels of Perfectionism include clerical jobs, managers, computer programmers, and mechanics. Low scorers may be found in artistic and creative jobs where there is a need for flexibility and creative thinking (Cattell & Schuerger, 2003).

Finally, the sixteenth factor is Tension (Q4). Low scorers are relaxed, tranquil, patient, and composed, but may not push themselves to get things accomplished. High scorers are tense, restless, driven, and easily annoyed (Walter, 2008). Tension correlates positively with the Big Five facet, Angry Hostility and negatively with Compliance (Conn & Rieke, 1994).

One might expect high scorers to dislike slow-paced classes that do not challenge them. On the other hand, low scorers might not want to undertake difficult learning tasks or challenging assignments. Cattell and Schuerger (2003) state that Tension is not a strong predictor of occupational choice, but an example of a high scoring occupation is an artist and a low-scoring occupation is a firefighter.

In addition to the sixteen primary factors, the 16PF measures five global factors derived from the primary scales. These factors correlate in expected directions with the Big Five personality factors (Cattell & Schuerger, 2003), but are not the focus of this book, since I found scores reported only for the 16 primary scales for engineers, scientists, and librarians.

3.3.2 The Big Five/Narrow Trait Framework (Personal Style Inventory)

The PSI has been used in studies of librarians', scientists', and engineers' personalities (Lounsbury et al., 2012; Williamson & Lounsbury, 2016; Williamson, Lounsbury, & Han, 2013; Williamson, Pemberton, & Lounsbury, 2005, 2008). It is a Big Five/Narrow Trait framework developed by John Lounsbury and Lucy Gibson (Lounsbury & Gibson, 2006). The Big Five traits included are similar to those developed by Costa and McCrae in the

Five Factor Model (Costa & McCrae, 1992), and they include Extraversion, Emotional Stability, Conscientiousness, Teamwork (Agreeableness), and Openness. In addition to these five traits, there are several narrow traits that pertain to work and academic behavior, such as Tough-Mindedness, Work Drive, Optimism, and Visionary Work Style. Lounsbury and Gibson added the narrow traits to their framework beyond the Big Five because they increased validity relationships (the variance that could be accounted for in addition to the Big Five traits), and they were empirically related to academic or work success (Landers & Lounsbury, 2006; Lounsbury & Gibson, 2006). The following list defines some of the traits in the PSI framework (Williamson et al., 2008).

(1) Adaptability. Flexibility and making adjustments to changes. High scorers function well with change and are adaptable. Low scorers are more rigid and like predictable work environments.

(2) Assertiveness. Forcefulness, taking charge of situations, speaking up.

(3) Autonomy. Self-directedness and preferring to make own decisions at work.

(4) Conscientiousness. Being organized, rule-following, and reliable.

(5) Customer service orientation. Putting the customer first even if the job does not require it; may refer to either internal or external customer service.

(6) Emotional resilience. Resilience to stress.

(7) Extraversion. Gregariousness, talkativeness, warm-heartedness, sociability.

(8) Openness. Receptiveness to new learning and experiences and innovation.

(9) Optimism. Hopefulness about people and the future and tendency to persist in the face of problems.

(10) Teamwork (Agreeableness). Cooperativeness in working in a team or group work.

(11) Tough-Mindedness. Making decisions and evaluating information based on logic and facts rather than intuition or feelings.

(12) Work drive. Investing extensive time and energy in work and willingness to extend oneself if necessary to achieve work goals.

(13) Visionary vs operational work style. Creating organizational vision, strategy, or long-term goals, versus focusing on day-to-day activities, problems, and goals.

The PSI and its related measures such as the Adolescent Personal Style Inventory have been used in a number of studies of academic success, sense of community, and self-directed or self-regulated learning (Kirwan, Lounsbury, & Gibson, 2014; Lounsbury, Levy, Park, Gibson, & Smith, 2009; Lounsbury, Loveland, & Gibson, 2003; Lounsbury, Sundstrom, Loveland, & Gibson, 2003; Ridgell & Lounsbury, 2004). An important variable in respect to library instruction is self-directed, or self-regulated learning, which is taking responsibility for one's own learning and regulating oneself to achieve learning objectives. Kirwan et al. found that several broad and narrow traits correlated significantly with self-regulated learning. The college students in this study's sample who scored high on self-regulated learning had higher Work Drive, Openness, satisfaction with their major, Sense of Identity, Optimism, Conscientiousness, Emotional Stability, and Agreeableness.

Another study of interest to science and engineering librarians was a comparison of the personality traits and major satisfaction of engineering students and students in two other majors. Williams (2009) found that engineering students were more tough-minded and emotionally stable than psychology and education students. Also engineering students' major satisfaction was positively correlated with Agreeableness, Conscientiousness, Emotional Stability, Openness, Optimism, Self-Directed Learning, Sense of Identity, and Work Drive. Major satisfaction was negatively correlated with Aggression.

3.4 CONCLUSION

As this chapter has shown, personality traits can contribute in several ways to teaching and learning. The 16PF and the PSI describe a range of characteristics that may play a part in library instruction to science and engineering students. As will be seen in the next chapter, librarians, scientists, and engineers have distinctive personality traits different from the norm averages as measured by the 16PF and the PSI. They also have distinctive Kolb learning styles. Once a librarian is aware of these typical characteristics, he or she can begin to form hypotheses about what to expect in the instructional settings with these groups of students.

REFERENCES

Caspi, A., Chajut, E., Saporta, K., & Beyth-Marom, R. (2006). The influence of personality on social participation in learning environments. *Learning and Individual Differences, 16*(2), 129–144. http://dx.doi.org/10.1016/j.lindif.2005.07.003.

Cattell, H. E., & Schuerger, J. M. (2003). *Essentials of 16PF assessment.* Hoboken, NJ: John Wiley & Sons.

Chamorro-Premuzic, T., & Furnham, A. (2009). Mainly Openness: The relationship between the Big Five personality traits and learning approaches. *Learning and Individual Differences, 19*(4), 524–529. http://dx.doi.org/10.1016/j.lindif.2009.06.004.

Clayson, D. E., & Sheffet, M. J. (2006). Personality and the student evaluation of teaching. *Journal of Marketing Education, 28*(2), 149–160. http://dx.doi.org/10.1177/0273475306288402.

Coaley, K. (2014). *An introduction to psychological assessment and psychometrics.* Los Angeles, CA: Sage.

Conn, S. R., & Rieke, M. L. (1994). *16PF fifth edition technical manual.* Champaign, IL: Institute for Personality and Ability Testing.

Cornelius-White, J. (2007). Learner-centered teacher-student relationships are effective: A meta-analysis. *Review of Educational Research, 77*(1), 113–143. http://dx.doi.org/10.3102/003465430298563.

Costa, P. T., & McCrae, R. R. (1992). *NEO Personality Inventory-Revised (NEO-PI-R).* Odessa, FL: Psychological Assessment Resources.

Douglas, H. E., Bore, M., & Munro, D. (2016). Coping with university education: The relationships of time management behaviour and work engagement with the five factor model aspects. *Learning and Individual Differences, 45*, 268–274. http://dx.doi.org/10.1016/j.lindif.2015.12.004.

Entwistle, N. J. (2013). *Styles of learning and teaching: An integrated outline of educational psychology for students, teachers and lecturers.* Hoboken, NJ: Taylor and Francis.

Erdle, S., Murray, H. G., & Rushton, J. P. (1985). Personality, classroom behavior, and student ratings of college teaching effectiveness: A path analysis. *Journal of Educational Psychology, 77*(4), 394. http://dx.doi.org/10.1037/0022-0663.77.4.394.

Furnham, A., & Medhurst, S. (1995). Personality correlates of academic seminar behaviour: A study of four instruments. *Personality and Individual Differences, 19*(2), 197–208. http://dx.doi.org/10.1016/0191-8869(95)00026-3.

Kirwan, J. R., Lounsbury, J. W., & Gibson, L. W. (2014). An investigation of the Big Five and narrow personality traits in relation to self-regulated learning. *Journal of Psychology and Behavioral Science, 2*(1), 1–11.

Kneipp, L. B., Kelly, K. E., Biscoe, J. D., & Richard, B. (2010). The impact of instructor's personality characteristics on quality of instruction. *College Student Journal, 44*(4), 901.

Landers, R. N., & Lounsbury, J. W. (2006). An investigation of Big Five and narrow personality traits in relation to internet usage. *Computers in Human Behavior, 22*(2), 283–293. http://dx.doi.org/10.1016/j.chb.2004.06.001.

Lounsbury, J. W., Foster, N., Patel, H., Carmody, P., Gibson, L. W., & Stairs, D. R. (2012). An investigation of the personality traits of scientists versus nonscientists and their relationship with career satisfaction. *R&D Management, 42*(1), 47–59. http://dx.doi.org/10.1111/j.1467-9310.2011.00665.x.

Lounsbury, J. W., & Gibson, L. W. (2006). *Personal style inventory: A personality measurement system for work and school settings.* Knoxville, TN: Resource Associates.

Lounsbury, J. W., Levy, J. J., Park, S.-H., Gibson, L. W., & Smith, R. (2009). An investigation of the construct validity of the personality trait of self-directed learning. *Learning and Individual Differences, 19*(4), 411–418. http://dx.doi.org/10.1016/j.lindif.2009.03.001.

Lounsbury, J. W., Loveland, J. M., & Gibson, L. W. (2003). An investigation of psychological sense of community in relation to Big Five personality traits. *Journal of Community Psychology, 31*(5), 531–541. http://dx.doi.org/10.1002/jcop.10065.

Lounsbury, J. W., Sundstrom, E., Loveland, J. M., & Gibson, L. W. (2003). Intelligence, "Big Five" personality traits, and work drive as predictors of course grade. *Personality and Individual Differences, 35*(6), 1231–1239. http://dx.doi.org/10.1016/S0191-8869(02)00330-6.

Patrick, C. L. (2011). Student evaluations of teaching: Effects of the Big Five personality traits, grades and the validity hypothesis. *Assessment & Evaluation in Higher Education, 36*(2), 239–249.

Patrick, B. C., Hisley, J., & Kempler, T. (2000). "What's everybody so excited about?": The effects of teacher enthusiasm on student intrinsic motivation and vitality. *The Journal of Experimental Education, 68*(3), 217–236. http://dx.doi.org/10.1080/00220970009600093.

Ridgell, S. D., & Lounsbury, J. W. (2004). Predicting academic success: General intelligence, "Big Five" personality traits, and work drive. *College Student Journal, 38*(4), 607.

Walter, V. (2008). *Manual for the 16PF career development report.* Champaign, IL: IPAT.

Williams, B. J. (2009). *Investigation of broad and narrow personality traits in relation to major satisfaction for students in engineering, education and psychology majors* [Honors thesis]. Knoxville, TN: University of Tennessee.

Williamson, J. M., & Lounsbury, J. W. (2016). Distinctive 16 PF personality traits of librarians. *Journal of Library Administration, 56*(2), 124–143. http://dx.doi.org/10.1080/01930826.2015.1105045.

Williamson, J. M., Lounsbury, J. W., & Han, L. D. (2013). Key personality traits of engineers for innovation and technology development. *Journal of Engineering and Technology Management, 30*(2), 157–168. http://dx.doi.org/10.1016/j.jengtecman.2013.01.003.

Williamson, J. M., Pemberton, A. E., & Lounsbury, J. W. (2005). An investigation of career and job satisfaction in relation to personality traits of information professionals. *The Library Quarterly, 75*(2), http://dx.doi.org/10.1086/431330.

Williamson, J. M., Pemberton, A. E., & Lounsbury, J. W. (2008). Personality traits of individuals in different specialties of librarianship. *Journal of Documentation, 64*(2), 273–286.

CHAPTER 4

Personality Traits and Learning Styles of Librarians, Scientists, and Engineers

4.1 16PF RESULTS

Williamson and Lounsbury (2016) found that librarians scored lower on Warmth (A), Emotional Stability (C), Dominance (E), Liveliness (F), Rule-Consciousness (G), Social Boldness (H), Vigilance (L), and Perfectionism (Q3) than a norm population. They scored higher than the norm population on Reasoning (B), Sensitivity (I), Abstractedness (M), Apprehension (O), Openness to Change (Q1), and Self-Reliance (Q2). There was no difference between librarians and the norm population on Privateness (N), and Tension (Q4).

Conn and Rieke (1994) reported the 16PF characteristics of scientists and engineers in the *16PF Fifth Edition Technical Manual*. Engineers scored higher than a norm population on Reasoning (B), Abstractedness (M), and Openness to Change (Q1). They scored lower on Emotional Stability (C), Rule-Consciousness (G), and Sensitivity (I).

Conn and Rieke (1994) reported that scientists scored higher than a norm population on Reasoning (B), Abstractedness (M), Openness to Change, and Self-Reliance (Q2); but lower on Emotional Stability (C), Liveliness (F), Rule-Consciousness (G), and Perfectionism (Q3).

Thus librarians share some traits with their science and engineering clientele. Like both engineers and scientists they had higher than average scores on Reasoning, Abstractedness, and Openness to Change. Like Scientists, they had higher than average Self-Reliance. Like both groups, they had lower than average Rule-Consciousness and Perfectionism, and like scientists, they had lower than average Liveliness.

Librarians scored lower than average on several traits that scientists and engineers scored in the average range: Warmth, Dominance, Social Boldness, and Vigilance. They scored higher than average on Sensitivity and Apprehension whereas engineers scored lower than average on Sensitivity

Teaching to Individual Differences in Science and Engineering Librarianship
http://dx.doi.org/10.1016/B978-0-08-101881-1.00004-2

and scientists scored in the average range on Sensitivity. Both scientists and engineers scored in the average range on Apprehension whereas librarians scored higher than average on this factor.

One would surmise, based on these results, that librarians might be shyer than engineers and scientists and more submissive, trusting, and anxious. The results also suggest that librarians would be less utilitarian and objective than engineers and scientists. I was unable to compare the groups directly using independent sample t tests[9] because the standard deviations were not available for the engineer and scientist groups in Conn and Rieke's results (1994). The independent sample t test requires means, sample sizes, and standard deviations.

The following traits seem germane to instruction:

High Reasoning. Scientists, engineers, and librarians are all able to understand complex information.

High Abstractedness. Scientists, engineers, and librarians all tend to get absorbed in ideas.

High Openness to Change. Scientists, engineers, and librarians all enjoy learning new information.

Low Rule-Consciousness and Perfectionism. Scientists, engineers, and librarians will have the capacity for flexible, creative thinking.

Low Sensitivity. Scientists and engineers will be drawn to logical reasoning and will have a utilitarian, objective approach.

High Sensitivity. Librarians will tend to be empathetic and have an aesthetic approach.

Low Warmth. Librarians may seem reserved when providing instruction.

Low Social Boldness. Librarians may be shy when providing instruction.

Low Emotional Stability. Scientists and engineers may feel stress in learning situations, and librarians may feel stress when providing instruction.

High Apprehension. Librarians may worry or feel anxiety when providing instruction.

16PF results were available for three samples of engineering and technology students at a northern US technical university (Smith, 2010).[10] The three student groups included:

---

[9]Independent sample t tests determine whether the difference between the scores from two samples is statistically significant. The means (average values) of the scores are used, as well as the standard deviations. The standard deviation indicates whether scores tend to be close to the mean, or more dispersed.

[10]The sample included some re-entry students in a remedial program. I do not know if this affected whether the personality scores of the students were typical for their majors.

College of Information Sciences (which was comprised of 67 students enrolled in Applied Networks & Systems, Information Technology, New Media Information Technology, Computer Science, and Software Engineering);

College of Applied Science and Technology (36 students in Applied Arts and Sciences, Packaging Science, Multidisciplinary, Pre-Med, Creative Writing Literature, Manufacturing Engineering Technology, Civil Engineering Technology, Electrical Engineering Technology, Mechanical Engineering Technology, and Computer Engineering Technology);

College of Engineering (49 students in Industrial Engineering, Computer Engineering, Mechanical Engineering, Electrical Engineering, and Undeclared Engineering).

The librarians in Williamson and Lounsbury's sample (2016) are less Dominant, Lively, Vigilant, Abstracted, and Private than the COIS students. They are more Rule-Conscious, Sensitive, Self-Reliant, and Perfectionistic than COIS students as well. Librarians are less Dominant, Lively, and Vigilant than the COAST students. They score higher on Reasoning, Sensitivity, and Self-Reliance than these students. The librarians score lower on Dominance, Liveliness, Vigilance, and Abstractedness than the COE students, but higher on Warmth, Sensitivity, and Self-Reliance.

These findings show that librarians have many personality differences with computer science and engineering students, although they share some similarities as well. Perhaps librarians' low Liveliness and high Sensitivity, compared to the students, are of most concern. It is possible that engineering and computer science students will perceive librarians as overly serious and not sufficiently objective and logical.

4.2 PERSONAL STYLE INVENTORY

Lounsbury and Gibson (2006) developed the Personal Style Inventory. The inventory has been administered to a number of occupational groups.

PSI results comparing engineers' and scientists' personality scores with those of people from other occupations were available. When compared with nonengineers, engineers scored lower on Assertiveness, Conscientiousness, Customer Service Orientation, Emotional Stability, Extraversion, Image Management, Optimism, Teamwork, Visionary Style, and Work Drive. They scored higher on Intrinsic Motivation and Tough-Mindedness (Williamson, Lounsbury, & Han, 2013). When scientists were compared with people from all other occupations, they scored lower than nonscientists on Conscientiousness, Emotional Stability, Extraversion, Assertiveness, Optimism, and Customer Service Orientation. They scored higher on Openness, Intrinsic Motivation, Tough-Mindedness, and Visionary Style (Lounsbury et al., 2012). Comparisons between librarians' PSI scores and those of nonlibrarians were not available, although Williamson, Lounsbury, and Pemberton found differences with respect to personality variables between librarians in different specialties (2008).

Overall, the PSI findings for scientists and engineers seem to be consistent with the 16PF results. Scientists and Engineers are low on Emotional Stability, Extraversion, and Conscientiousness (which is similar to Rule-Consciousness and Perfectionism). They are high on Tough-Mindedness, which is similar to having low Sensitivity. The PSI adds information about personality variables not available in the 16PF, such as Customer Service Orientation, Image Management, Optimism, Work Drive, Visionary Style, and Intrinsic Motivation.

The following PSI traits seem to be germane to instruction:

Low Conscientiousness. Scientists and engineers may have the capacity for flexible, creative thinking.

Low Emotional Stability. Scientists and engineers may feel stress in learning situations.

Low Extraversion. Scientists and engineers may be reserved and not enjoy participating in large group discussions.

Low Optimism. Scientists and engineers may have a pessimistic outlook.

High Intrinsic Motivation. Scientists and engineers may be motivated by inherent interest in a topic, rather than primarily extrinsic rewards.

High Tough-Mindedness. Scientists and engineers may have an objective, logical approach.

High Openness. Scientists may be open to new learning.

These findings are consistent with the 16PF scores of scientists, engineers, engineering students, and computer science students discussed above. STEM librarians can infer that their students on average will be logical, creative, introverted, highly motivated by intrinsic interest in their subjects, and at times emotionally reactive.

4.3 KOLB LEARNING STYLES

I could locate only one study of the Kolb learning styles of librarians (Choi, 1989). In a study of public services and technical services librarians, Choi found that 38.6% of the librarians were Assimilators, 27.1% were Convergers, 19.3% were Divergers, and 15% were Accommodators. Choi found it interesting that even though 72.1% of the librarians had majored in humanities or liberal arts, they did not fall into the expected Diverger category that is common among most liberal arts and humanities majors. Overall, the majority of the librarians preferred Abstract Conceptualization.

I would expect science and engineering librarians to prefer Abstract Conceptualization for the most part, as well, given that they probably are interested in the subject matter of their clientele, which is abstract. Scientists and engineers overwhelmingly prefer Abstract Conceptualization. Kolb and Kolb found that those with educational specializations in engineering, science, and mathematics tended to score most frequently in the Analyzing, Thinking, and Deciding styles on the 2013 KLSI 4.0 (2013). These would have been Assimilators and Convergers in the earlier Learning Styles Inventory. Analyzers strongly prefer Reflective Observation and Abstract Conceptualization. Thinkers prefer Abstract Conceptualization and balance Reflective Observation and Active Experimentation. Deciders prefer Abstract Conceptualization and Active Experimentation. Individuals with a specialization in computer science/information science tended to also be Analyzers, Thinkers, and Deciders, but many also preferred the balanced style combining Abstract Conceptualization, Concrete Experience, Reflective Observation, and Active Experimentation.

If librarians share the same learning styles as engineers and scientists for the most part, then they may select instructional activities such as lectures and hands-on practice that would be preferred by engineering and science students. The main possibility for mismatch that I can see is that librarians may in some cases have a more reflective style than those students who prefer Active Experimentation. I believe that it is important for librarians to incorporate active learning activities or total participation techniques to keep these students engaged. Also, those librarians who prefer Concrete Experience may not gravitate naturally to the abstract thinking style that science and engineering students tend to prefer.

4.4 CONNECTING WITH DIVERSE AUDIENCES

Although engineers and scientists tend to have distinctive personality traits and learning styles compared to norm groups, factors such as nationality, gender, and race may slightly affect personality and learning style characteristics, as well. This section, written from the point of view of an engineering librarian in the United States, describes important characteristics of international students, female students, male students, and students of different US races and ethnicities. As will be seen, there have been studies of personality and learning style characteristics of these different populations, but it is also important to be aware that personality and learning style differences between groups may not be as large as differences within groups. Also, the librarian needs to be aware of the fact that personality traits and learning styles may be expressed in different ways in different groups. For example, Agreeableness (which is composed of the aspects, Compassion and Politeness, and additional facets described in Chapter 3) may be expressed in different ways by males than females due to gender roles.

4.4.1 International Students

A report of the Student and Exchange Visitor Program of the US Immigration and Customs Enforcement department stated that there were 466,964 F and M international students studying in STEM majors in the United States during July, 2016 (Student Exchange and Visitor Program, 2016).[11] Also, 406,732 of these students were from Asian countries. The most STEM students came from India, and 68% of the international students in mathematics and statistics were from China. Sixty-nine percent of the international STEM students were male.

To take a statistic from the institution where I work, in Fall 2015, 40% of the Masters and Doctorate students in the Tickle College of Engineering at the University of Tennessee Knoxville were nonresident aliens (University of Tennessee Office of Institutional Research and Assessment, 2016). Twenty-four percent of the Natural Sciences Masters and Doctorate students were nonresident aliens. By contrast, only about 2% of the undergraduate students in the engineering and the natural sciences were nonresident aliens. Given these statistics, it behooves science and engineering librarians to learn about characteristics of international students, particularly graduate students.

4.4.1.1 Personality Characteristics

Studies that report on the characteristics of individuals in different countries yield valuable data about the populations of STEM graduate students. Jackson and Wang compared Chinese and US college students on the Big Five personality traits (2013). The authors found that Chinese students were less Extraverted, less Neurotic, and less Open to Experience than US students, but more Conscientious. McCrae and Terracciano (2005) collected

---

[11]F and M students are in academic and vocational programs, respectively. Different requirements apply to these categories; for example, F students can take an annual vacation, while M students cannot.

observer ratings to compare cultures and found that Hong Kong Chinese individuals were more Neurotic and less Extraverted, less Agreeable, and less Open to Experience than Americans. In a study of how individuals described their personalities in 56 countries, individuals from Hong Kong China rated themselves as more Neurotic and less Extraverted, Agreeable, Open, and Conscientious than US individuals did (Schmitt, Allik, McCrae, & Benet-Martinez, 2007). The authors make the point that the unexpectedly low scores on Conscientiousness found in East Asian cultures may be due to these cultures' having very high cultural standards for Conscientiousness:

> *That is, certain norms may establish how punctual, strong-willed, and reliable people are expected to be in different cultures. Suppose, for example, that there are different cultural standards for being organized, purposeful, and achievement oriented. Let us imagine a culture where these standards are set extremely high and almost every effort falls short of these almost compulsive demands. Compared with these standards, almost everyone is forced to report on a self-report scale that he or she is less organized and determined than is generally the case in this particular culture.*

Individuals from India rated themselves as less Extraverted, Conscientious, and Open than people in the US samples did (Schmitt et al., 2007). Migliore (2011) investigated whether Five Factor Model (Big Five) personality traits in Indian academically trained professionals were correlated with Hofstede, Hofstede, & Minkov's cultural dimensions, which are used to compare cultures (2010). Table 4.1 summarizes the Hofstede et al. cultural dimensions.

Academically trained professionals in India rated themselves as having a lower long-term orientation than academically trained professionals in the United States (Migliore, 2011). People with a long-term orientation are more willing to accept delayed gratification of needs than those with a short-term orientation. To give another cultural difference, China is a more collectivistic culture than the United States. Individuals in China tend to value friends, family, and groups more than the self (Jackson and Wang, 2013). Migliore (2011) found only one significant correlation between Big Five personality traits and Hofstede et al.'s dimensions. Extraversion was negatively correlated with individualism in a manager sample used in the study.

4.4.1.2 Learning Styles

Joy and Kolb (2009), in a study including more than 500 participants from seven countries, found that culture had a small effect on the Abstract Conceptualization/Concrete Experience dimension of the Kolb Learning Styles Inventory. When the scores of individuals from different countries were

Table 4.1 Hofstede et al.'s cultural dimensions

Cultural dimension	Description
Individualism/Collectivism	Self or family-focused vs people-group-focused
Power Distance	Extent to which less powerful members of a culture accept unequal distribution of power
Masculinity-Femininity	Clear gender roles vs overlapping gender roles
Uncertainty Avoidance	Extent to which members of culture are threatened by uncertain or ambiguous situations
Time Orientation (long term vs short term)	Accept or do not accept delayed gratification

Source: Based on Migliore's summary (Migliore, L. A. (2011). Relation between Big Five personality traits and hofstede's cultural dimensions: Samples from the USA and India. *Cross Cultural Management: An International Journal, 18*(1), 38–54. doi:10.1108/13527601111104287) of the Hofstede et al. dimensions.

examined, the authors found that the United States was in the Diverging quadrant; Singapore and Germany were in the Assimilating quadrant; India was in the Converging quadrant; and Poland, Italy, and Brazil were in the Accommodating quadrant. The effect of culture was smaller than that of academic specialization, but larger than that of gender.

Some dimensions of culture, such as uncertainty avoidance also had an effect on Kolb learning style dimension scores. For example, those with high uncertainty avoidance scored higher on Abstract Conceptualization than Concrete Experience, and higher on Reflective Observation than Active Experimentation. To give another example, individuals who were high on future orientation scored higher on Abstract Conceptualization than Concrete Experience.[12]

Joy and Kolb (2009) caution that the respondents from different cultures in the study were limited to computer literate individuals who were able to read English. The true influence of culture on learning style dimension scores may have been underestimated. Since the effect of culture was smaller than that of academic specialization, it may be the case that engineering and science students from different countries will tend to have similar learning styles

4.4.1.3 Other Factors

In addition to possibly having some personality differences, learning style differences, and cultural differences such as those discussed by Hofstede et al. (2010), international students also may be nonnative English speakers and in some cases may have different information literacy backgrounds

[12]See additional findings in the original article.

than United States students. In other cases, their level of information literacy may be comparable to that of students from the United States. Jabeen, Yun, Rafiq, Jabeen, and Tahir (2016) found that 100% of the University libraries in Beijing offered training on introductory skills in information literacy, as well as library tours and orientations. Forty percent of University libraries offered information literacy training in advanced information skills and research-level skills. Given this statistic, Chinese students may have as much information literacy training as many US students entering graduate programs.

Ghosh and Ghosh (2009) discuss several developments in India since 2000 that are increasing its progress as a knowledge economy. National information centers have been set up to supply information to Indian scientists in many disciplines, and there is also a Digital Library of India with more than a million books in several Indian languages. As in many other countries, there is a digital divide between those with access to Internet communication technologies, and those that do not have this access.

Other cultures might be discussed besides China and India, but these two examples show that there are differences to consider when teaching international students, in addition to differences in personality characteristics and learning styles that the librarian might encounter with any student. In addition, the librarian should realize that expression of personality characteristics may differ in different cultures.

4.4.2 Gender
4.4.2.1 Personality Characteristics
Librarians teach both female and male science and engineering students, and they may find differences in their personality characteristics, on average. These may be small effects, however. Costa, Terracciano, and McCrae (2001) examined gender differences on the NEO-PI-R Big Five personality dimensions from 26 cultures. None of the effects was huge: "Gender differences, although pervasive, appear to be relatively subtle compared with the range of individual differences found within each gender." The differences also appeared to be pan-cultural, with United States gender differences being fairly similar to those in the other cultures.

Women were more Neurotic and Agreeable than men. They also tended to be higher than men in the Extraversion facets, Warmth, Positive Emotions, and Gregariousness. They scored lower on the Extraversion facets, Assertiveness and Excitement Seeking. Women scored higher than men on the Openness to Experience facets, Openness to Feeling, Actions, and Aesthetics, but lower on Openness to Ideas. They scored higher than men on the Conscientiousness facet, Dutifulness.

Weisberg, DeYoung, and Hirsh (2011) found differences between 2643 women and men in aspects of the Big Five dimensions. There are two aspects for each of the five factors of Neuroticism, Extraversion, Openness, Agreeableness, and Conscientiousness.[13] These subfactors include Enthusiasm and Assertiveness (E), Politeness and Compassion (A), Industriousness and Orderliness (C), Volatility and Withdrawal (N), and Openness and Intellect (O). Women scored significantly higher than men on Enthusiasm, Compassion, Politeness, Orderliness, Volatility, Withdrawal, and Openness, as well as on the larger factors, Extraversion, Agreeableness, and Neuroticism. They scored lower than men on the aspects of Assertiveness and Intellect.

These findings are consistent with those of Costa et al. (2001). Both studies show that women on average are more Agreeable and Neurotic than men (on all facets and both aspects), but are less Assertive and Open to Ideas. Since the differences are small (Costa et al., 2001), it may be unadvisable to draw sweeping conclusions about gender differences in personality. At the same time, being aware that female students may differ slightly in personality from male students may make librarians more sensitive to personal factors affecting the educational experience of these women, who are minorities in the fields of science and engineering. The National Science Foundation (2015) reported that in 2012, 80.8% of undergraduates enrolled in engineering programs in the United States were male and 19.2% were female.

4.4.2.2 Learning Styles

Kolb and Kolb (2013) found that women were less abstract than men on the Abstract Conceptualization-Concrete Experience dimension of the Kolb Learning Styles Index 4.0, but there was no gender difference in respect to the Active Experimentation-Reflective Observation dimension. Kolb and Kolb make the point; however, that it is not warranted to state stereotypes such as women are concrete and men are abstract, "since mean differences are statistically significant but there is considerable overlap between male and female distributions on AC–CE and AE–RO."

---

[13]See Table 3.1 in Chapter 3.

4.4.3 US Racial Groups

The National Science Foundation (2015) found that about 12% of students who earned bachelor's degrees in engineering were from underrepresented minority groups. By way of comparison, underrepresented minority groups make up 12.6% of students who earned bachelor's degrees in the physical science, 19.4% of students who earned degrees in computer science, and 15.1% of students who earned degrees in biological sciences. In 2014, 61.5% of students who earned bachelor's degrees in science and engineering fields were white, 12.1% were Hispanic or Latino, 9.5% were Asian, and 8.7% were Black or African American (National Science Foundation, 2015). (These were the four largest groups.)

Foldes, Duehr, and Ones (2008) did a metaanalysis[14] of previous reports of Big Five personality characteristics of US racial groups and found some differences at the global factor level (Emotional Stability, Extraversion, and Agreeableness, for example) and at the facet level. An example of a facet of Extraversion is Sociability. Foldes et al.'s purpose was to determine if selecting individuals for jobs based on personality traits could result in adverse impact against any racial groups, which is prohibited by the Civil Rights Act of 1991.

The authors found some small to moderate differences in personality characteristics that they calculated could produce adverse impact in some cases. I report here on the moderate facet-level differences and overall factor differences between racial groups:

1. Whites scored higher than Blacks on Extraversion.
2. There was a moderate difference on the Extraversion facet Sociability, with Whites scoring higher than Blacks.
3. There were modest differences between Blacks and Whites on Emotional Stability and some of its facets.
4. There were only small differences between Blacks and Whites on Conscientiousness.
5. Whites scored slightly higher on Emotional Stability than Asians.
6. Whites scored moderately higher on Even-Temperedness than Asians.
7. Asians scored moderately higher on Self-Esteem and Low Anxiety than Whites.
8. Asians scored higher than Whites on Agreeableness.
9. Asians scored higher than Whites on the Conscientiousness facet Order.

---

[14]A meta-analysis statistically analyzes other studies to see if overall conclusions can be drawn about various findings.

10. Hispanics scored slightly higher than Whites on the Emotional Stability facets Self-Esteem and Low Anxiety.
11. Whites scored higher than American Indians on Extraversion.
12. Whites scored higher than American Indians on Emotional Stability.
13. Whites scored higher than American Indians on Agreeableness.
14. American Indians scored higher than Whites on Conscientiousness.
15. Blacks scored higher than Asians on Extraversion, and its facets, Dominance and Sociability.
16. Blacks scored higher than Asians on Emotional Stability and its facet, Even-Temperedness.
17. Hispanics scored higher than Blacks on the Extraversion facet, Sociability.

As can be seen, these findings are piecemeal and the authors caution that between-group differences are smaller than within-group differences. They make the point:

> Studying race differences in personality is socially controversial, scientifically complex, and practically important. The more extensive our knowledge, the greater our understanding of what, if anything, should be done to ensure that such differences do not adversely affect individual racial groups or the fair use of personality measures in selection.

I could not locate any metaanalytic studies of Kolb learning styles of US racial groups. It is thus impossible to make any generalizations about differences between racial groups on the Kolb learning styles dimensions, since differences between groups are often smaller than within groups.

The librarian providing instruction to science and engineering students should be careful not to stereotype members of racial groups, genders, or nationalities with respect to personality characteristics or learning styles.

4.4.4 Forming a Connection With a Range of Students

Recognizing that every student is different, the librarian needs to find a way to engage individuals with many personality traits and learning styles. Engagement is particularly important in library instruction because the librarian may see the students only on the occasion of the instruction, and he or she needs to encourage students to seek help later, as well as to learn important skills. The librarian needs to display behaviors that students can relate to, even if the librarian is naturally Introverted or Apprehensive.

A librarian can demonstrate willingness to help by tailoring the instruction to the assignment or to tasks the students must accomplish. Librarians can anticipate students' needs and try to provide resources that will help. Audience analysis based on familiarity with the course and the curriculum is important. Demonstrating that he or she is aware of the tasks the students have to do will help the librarian form a connection with students who have many personality traits and learning styles.

Along with analyzing the tasks that the students have to do, either by talking with the instructor or based on experience, the librarian can try to imagine how these tasks will affect different kinds of students. For example, realizing that there were many international graduate students at my university, I sought out tools to help out with English usage and editing manuscripts, since writing can be a challenge for these nonnative speakers. Similarly, the librarian can think about how various required tasks may affect students who have different kinds of personality traits or learning styles.

To give just a few examples:

Students with low Emotional Stability would be expected to have difficulty with challenging tasks that are tied to a grade. They might also be affected by time pressure. Help for them could include introducing them to handbooks that will show them how to solve problems, offering individual consultations, and being familiar with the range of campus resources that could help such students, such as tutoring.

Students who are low on Social Boldness would be expected to have problems with making presentations until they get experience. The librarian could compile a list of resources on public speaking, tell students about practice presentation rooms, and offer to help students find sources for their presentations.

Students who strongly prefer Concrete Experience may not enjoy abstract lecture classes. The librarian can direct students to handbooks that provide concrete examples in worked problems. The librarian might also encourage students to sign up for current technology blogs or RSS feeds so that they can see concrete examples of abstract principles they may be learning about in their classes.

Highly Self-Reliant students and students low on Social Boldness may not want to consult with a librarian in person. The librarian can help by having chat office hours and creating web pages that enable the students to work independently without face-to-face instruction.

Students who are low on aspects of Conscientiousness, especially Order (Perfectionism on the 16PF), may have organizational difficulties. The librarian could help by providing checklists for steps in finding and citing sources. Also, the librarian could provide end of the semester workshops for students who have waited until the last minute to complete departmental continuing education requirements. The librarian could also provide a data literacy component to design classes so that students will learn how to organize their data in a beneficial way.

Many of the things librarians already do can be beneficial to a wide range of students. Knowledge of how personality and learning styles impact learning can help a librarian think of more ways to be helpful and anticipate student needs.

4.5 CONCLUSION

This chapter has shown that academic specialization in science and engineering is associated with distinctive personality and learning style profiles. County of origin, gender, and racial/ethnic background may also have a small impact on personality. The librarian, realizing that students are diverse in many characteristics, should seek a way to make a connection with them, for example, by tailoring instruction to assignments and student needs.

REFERENCES

Choi, J. M. (1989). Learning styles of academic librarians. *College & Research Libraries, 50*, 691–699. http://dx.doi.org/10.5860/crl_50_06_691.

Conn, S. R., & Rieke, M. L. (1994). *16PF fifth edition technical manual*. Champaign, IL: Institute for Personality and Ability Testing.

Costa, P. T., Terracciano, A., & McCrae, R. R. (2001). Gender differences in personality traits across cultures: Robust and surprising findings. *Journal of Personality and Social Psychology, 81*(2), 322. http://dx.doi.org/10.1037/0022-3514.81.2.322.

Foldes, H. J., Duehr, E. E., & Ones, D. S. (2008). Group differences in personality: Meta-analyses comparing five us racial groups. *Personnel Psychology, 61*(3), 579–616. http://dx.doi.org/10.1111/j.1744-6570.2008.00123.x.

Ghosh, M., & Ghosh, I. (2009). ICT and information strategies for a knowledge economy: The Indian experience. *Program, 43*(2), 187–201. http://dx.doi.org/10.1108/00330330910954398.

Hofstede, G., Hofstede, G. J., & Minkov, M. 2010. Intercultural cooperation and its importance for survival. *Cultures and organizations, software of the mind*. New York: McGraw-Hill.

Jabeen, M., Yun, L., Rafiq, M., Jabeen, M., & Tahir, M. A. (2016). Information literacy in academic and research libraries of Beijing, China practices, methods and problems. *Information Development, 32*(3), 579–591. http://dx.doi.org/10.1177/0266666914562845.

Jackson, L. A., & Wang, J.-L. (2013). Cultural differences in social networking site use: A comparative study of china and the united states. *Computers in Human Behavior, 29*(3), 910–921. http://dx.doi.org/10.1016/j.chb.2012.11.024.

Joy, S., & Kolb, D. A. (2009). Are there cultural differences in learning style? *International Journal of Intercultural Relations, 33*(1), 69–85. http://dx.doi.org/10.1016/j.ijintrel.2008.11.002.

Kolb, A. Y., & Kolb, D. A. (2013). *The Kolb Learning Style Inventory 4.0: A comprehensive guide to the theory, psychometrics, research on validity and educational applications*. Experience Based Learning Systems, Inc.

Lounsbury, J. W., Foster, N., Patel, H., Carmody, P., Gibson, L. W., & Stairs, D. R. (2012). An investigation of the personality traits of scientists versus nonscientists and their relationship with career satisfaction. *R&D Management, 42*(1), 47–59. http://dx.doi.org/10.1111/j.1467-9310.2011.00665.x.

Lounsbury, J. W., & Gibson, L. W. (2006). *Personal style inventory: A personality measurement system for work and school settings.* Knoxville, TN: Resource Associates.

McCrae, R. R., & Terracciano, A. (2005). Personality profiles of cultures: Aggregate personality traits. *Journal of Personality and Social Psychology, 89*(3), 407. http://dx.doi.org/10.1037/0022-3514.89.3.407.

Migliore, L. A. (2011). Relation between Big Five personality traits and Hofstede's cultural dimensions: Samples from the USA and India. *Cross Cultural Management: An International Journal, 18*(1), 38–54. http://dx.doi.org/10.1108/13527601111104287.

National Science Foundation. (2015). *Women, minorities, and persons with disabilities in science and engineering.* Retrieved from https://www.nsf.gov/statistics/2015/nsf15311/start.cfm.

Schmitt, D. P., Allik, J., McCrae, R. R., & Benet-Martinez, V. (2007). The geographic distribution of Big Five personality traits: Patterns and profiles of human self-description across 56 nations. *Journal of Cross-Cultural Psychology, 38*(2), 173–212. http://dx.doi.org/10.1177/0022022106297299.

Smith, J. 2010. *Differences in personality factors and college major choice. (M.S.).* New York: Rochester Institute of Technology.

Student Exchange and Visitor Program. (2016). *Student and exchange visitor information system: Sevis by the numbers general summary quarterly review.* July 2016. Retrieved from https://studyinthestates.dhs.gov/sevis-by-the-numbers.

University of Tennessee Office of Institutional Research and Assessment. (2016). *OIRA online reporting.* Retrieved from https://oira.utk.edu/onlineReporting.

Weisberg, Y. J., DeYoung, C. G., & Hirsh, J. B. (2011). Gender differences in personality across the ten aspects of the Big Five. *Frontiers in Psychology, 2*, 178. http://dx.doi.org/10.3389/fpsyg.2011.00178.

Williamson, J. M., & Lounsbury, J. W. (2016). Distinctive 16 PF personality traits of librarians. *Journal of Library Administration, 56*(2), 124–143. http://dx.doi.org/10.1080/01930826.2015.1105045.

Williamson, J. M., Lounsbury, J. W., & Han, L. D. (2013). Key personality traits of engineers for innovation and technology development. *Journal of Engineering and Technology Management, 30*(2), 157–168. http://dx.doi.org/10.1016/j.jengtecman.2013.01.003.

Williamson, J. M., Pemberton, A. E., & Lounsbury, J. W. (2008). Personality traits of individuals in different specialties of librarianship. *Journal of Documentation, 64*(2), 273–286.

CHAPTER 5

The Matching Approach

As I see it, matching can take three forms:

1. offer instruction that appeals to multiple learning styles or personality characteristics in a class (the well-balanced approach)
2. appeal to the "average" or predominant learning styles or personality characteristics of students (the stereotypical profile approach)
3. adapt to student characteristics that are assessed informally before or during instruction

Each of these approaches has potential benefits and drawbacks for science and engineering library instruction.

5.1 THE WELL-BALANCED APPROACH

Appealing to multiple learning styles or personality characteristics in a class seems to be the approach of "differentiated classrooms," where learning alternatives are presented for different students in a course (Tomlinson, 2014), as well as instructional designs for individual classes offering a variety of learning activities for different kinds of learners. Establishing differentiated classrooms seems to be germane to instructors who have long-term contact with the same students, such as over the course of a semester or a year. A librarian who meets with students for only one or a few times could not be expected to establish a differentiated classroom. The librarian does not know the learning styles or personality characteristics of individual students and thus could not mindfully tailor instruction to particular individuals. The librarian does not have the luxury of giving students learning styles inventories or personality assessments as perhaps some regular classroom instructor could do.

On the other hand, the librarian can offer a variety of learning activities for different kinds of learners. This approach would presumably offer "something for everybody," appealing at different times to students with different characteristics. "Teaching around the learning cycle" is an example of this kind of instruction. Several instructors who have applied

Teaching to Individual Differences in Science and Engineering Librarianship
http://dx.doi.org/10.1016/B978-0-08-101881-1.00005-4

Kolb's learning styles theory incorporate activities in their instruction that correspond to the four quadrants of his framework, hoping to address all parts of the learning cycle. Kolb stated that learning might not always proceed in order through the stages of Concrete Experience, Reflective Observation, Abstract Conceptualization, Active Experimentation, and then back to Concrete Experience (2015). Nevertheless, some lesson plans, such as those created using the 4MAT system, incorporate the idealized learning cycle, providing activities for these stages in order (McCarthy & McCarthy, 2006).

Similarly, one might include instructional activities for individuals with different personality characteristics. One could include participation techniques that would be comfortable for Introverts and Extraverts, such as Think-Share-Pairs, which would most likely be comfortable for introverts, and a larger class discussion, which would most likely be favored by Extraverts.

There are several benefits of the well-balanced approach. It provides a variety of instructional activities, which tends to make instruction more interesting. It also recognizes the diversity of individuals who make up a class. Finally, it is a holistic approach to instruction that takes into account several elements involved in the teaching and learning process.

5.1.1 Variety

Tewell (2014), in an engaging *C&RL News* article comparing stand-up comedy to library instruction, says that it is important to use a variety of instructional methods in a class, just as stand-up comedians vary their delivery within a performance.

> Different teaching methods will be appropriate for different messages. A task that students often find challenging, such as selecting pertinent keywords for searches, could be made easier and more fun by drawing concept maps on an easel pad a la Martin's approach. Depending on your objectives you may choose to integrate clickers, an interactive game, or a chalkboard into instruction sessions, but Martin demonstrates that the key is to use a variety of methods to reach the audience's diverse learning styles and keep them involved.

Similarly, Dabbour (1997) recommended adding active learning techniques to a freshman information literacy seminar, because these techniques appeal to a greater variety of learning styles than standard lectures, which appeal mostly to more self-directed learners.

While there are many resources that show librarians ways to vary their instructional activities, I will mention two here. First, Beard (2010) wrote

The Experiential Learning Toolkit: Blending Practice with Concepts. This book does not describe instructional activities specifically geared to information literacy classes, but it can give librarians much food for thought. As Beard states,

> *The possibilities of learning experiences are limitless, and in this sense this book is not, and certainly never set out to be a complete work. It is designed to encourage the evolution of practice to develop learning approaches that solve complex challenges in life, to make new additions to the vast range of concepts that underpin experiential learning. (p. 32)*

Beard presents an instructional model of attending to the whole person, which I will discuss further in Section 5.1.3. Class activities may be associated with six core dimensions of learning: Belonging, Doing, Sensing, Feeling, Knowing, and Being. An example of a Belonging activity is 1.4, "Different Ways to Know." The Belonging dimension has to do with space, and this activity involves movement of knowledge in a space, resulting in a new perspective. Students are given a group of printed images and explore producing trends, clusters, clusters of clusters, and analytical commentaries. This exercise develops analysis, synthesis, and evaluation skills. The exercise encourages students to engage actively with learning materials by reorganizing them in space, rather than just passively viewing images.

This exercise could be adapted for information literacy instruction if students were given cards with search terms or images and asked to come up with different clusters, or clusters of clusters of them in a mind map. Spatial reorganization of concepts expressed by search terms or labeled images could lead to a rich awareness of approaches one could use in generating search vocabulary. It could also emphasize to students how useful it might be to create a mind map when planning a search.

One could adapt other activities in Beard's book, such as 2.5, "Hearing Voices." This activity is associated with the Doing dimension and involves observing and then modeling various customer service scenarios. The activity could be adapted to engineering design classes in which students must learn how to elicit information about customers' needs. Nelson's chapter in *Integrating Information into the Engineering Design Process*, "Find the Real Need," contains a similar exercise in which students practice eliciting information in interviews (2014). To slightly adapt this exercise, one could have students watch a short video of an information-eliciting interview before practicing these skills with each other.

Another activity in Beard's toolkit is 4.3, "Re-framing, rewriting, and rethinking," which is associated with the Feeling dimension. In this activity students learn to re-frame and rewrite "scripts" in their mind having to do with negative thought patterns. While this might seem a bit too much like therapy to the engineering or science librarian, it could potentially be useful in addressing library anxiety. For example, the librarian could elicit or provide re-frames of such statements as:

I always find too much information in my search results.
Some of the "irrelevant" results I find contribute to my larger understanding of a topic and suggest new search terms to use. Also I can consult with a librarian about improving my search.

While Beard's activities may not seem immediately applicable to science and engineering library instruction, they do give the librarian the idea that varying instructional activities is important and that it can be done in very creative ways.

Another useful book about introducing variety into instruction is *Total Participation Techniques: Making Every Student an Active Learner* (Himmele & Himmele, 2011). This book aims to create engagement in all the students in a class. The authors state that the participation techniques can be applied in classes for all ages although I believe some of them would have to be adapted to be relevant to college students. The authors make the point that often class discussion opportunities in classes only elicit the cognitive engagement of the few students who answer the teacher's questions. Total participation techniques, on the other hand, involve all the students in a class. Examples of Total Participation Techniques that could be adapted to science and engineering library instruction include Think-Pair-Shares, Quick-Writes, Quick-Draws, Chalkboard Splash, Similes, Ranking, and Thumb Up/Down Votes.

Of these activities, Chalkboard Splash and Thumb Up/Down Votes may not be familiar to librarians. Chalkboard Splash is an activity where all the students in the class write an answer to a prompt on a chalkboard or whiteboard. This might not work for larger classes, but an analogous activity is possible in online classes if the teacher asks a question and requires everyone to respond. The Thumb Up/Down Votes activity prompts students to respond yes or no to a question and could readily be modified to use clickers.

Quick-Draws encourage students to make a quick diagram in response to a question. Quick-Writes are similar to minute papers. Think-Pair-Shares have students turn to the person next to them to discuss a question, and then there is some general reporting back to the larger group. Similes are designed to encourage students' analogous thinking in generating similarities to a prompted concept. Ranking gives students a list of items and asks them to rank them.

A nice thing about total participation techniques is that they have the potential for engaging students with a variety of personality characteristics and learning styles. Think-Pair-Shares, for example, should be less intimidating to shyer students than large class discussions. Similarly, clickers allow a certain anonymity to students' responses, while still involving everyone. Quick-Writes allow more reflective students to engage with material, but could also be appealing to active learners, since they must produce something with the act of writing. Most of the activities are free form enough that they could appeal to a variety of learners.

One may contrast these total participation techniques with instruction that singles out individuals. Singling out students can potentially be stressful for them, particularly if they are low on Emotional Stability, high on Apprehension, or highly Introverted. Total participation techniques also give the librarian useful feedback about how the class is going and help to form a connection between the librarian and students.

5.1.2 Diversity

The well-balanced approach recognizes that there are a variety of learning styles and personality characteristics among students in any class. Classes are never completely homogeneous, even if there is a "stereotypical profile" of personality traits and learning styles of engineering or science students. While the phenomena of accentuation of learning styles and person-environment fit do contribute to some similarities among individuals in a major or occupation, one should remember that particularly at lower levels of engineering and science classes, the learning styles accentuation process may not have taken place yet. Also, science classes often contain students from many majors at the lower levels, so one could expect to see a variety of personality and learning characteristics among the students. It is interesting to note that students with "nontypical" personality characteristics or learning styles—that is not typical to engineering—may not be retained in engineering (Rosati, 1993). It may be to engineering programs' advantage to encourage the retention of these students through inclusive instructional design.

5.1.3 Holism

Another nice feature of the well-balanced approach is that it is holistic. For example, Kolb conceptualized the learning cycle as moving through four stages for all individuals (2015). Thus during the learning process, individuals would have to use Concrete Experience, Reflective Observation, Abstract Conceptualization, and Active Experimentation. Incorporating activities for each of these stages would presumably support the entire, holistic learning cycle. Similarly, Beard viewed experiential learning as a holistic process involving multiple aspects (2010). Incorporating activities for each dimension (i.e., social, physical, and emotional) would facilitate a holistic learning process.

In the same way, accommodating multiple personality characteristics in instruction is advantageous from a holistic standpoint, as people behave:

at times in Introverted ways, at times in Extraverted ways,

at times in Emotionally Stable ways, at times in Neurotic ways,

at times in serious ways, at times in Lively ways,

and so forth. Personality scores such as low Introversion do not mean that the person does not ever enjoy Extraverted activities, just that he or she tends to enjoy introverted activities more often.

5.2 THE STEREOTYPICAL PROFILE APPROACH

Advocating the use of average profiles of *group* characteristics in a book about *individual* differences may seem like an oxymoron. Is it not the importance of individual differences to allow one to describe the diversity of human beings? Nevertheless, I believe that awareness of engineering and science students' typical personality and learning style profiles can inform library instruction in helpful ways.

First, the librarian going into an engineering or science class may know few to none of the students, and he or she may never see them again (in the worst case scenario). In this kind of situation, it may be helpful for the librarian to have some expectations about what the students will be like going in. If the librarian knows that *in general* many students may be more Introverted, Open to Change, have lower scores than the norm population on Emotional Stability, and that they may prefer abstract learning, than he or she can plan for encountering these characteristics. The "stereotypical profile" functions as a general heuristic the librarian may want to use when planning instruction. Naturally the librarian will need to keep in mind that this stereotypical profile is a simplification serving to give him or her some expectations going into a situation where little is known about the audience.

Of course, assumptions about students can have an effect on their learning, as studies of "self-fulfilling prophecies" in education show (Jussim, 1986).

Assuming at the outset that students will be low on resilience (Emotional Stability) may not be a good thing, as it may cause the librarian to overcompensate and not adequately stretch students. Also if the librarian assumes, say, that the students will be high on Openness to Change and attempts to engage their interest by introducing them to new databases and other tools, he or she will probably be correct about many students, but not others. Some students may be resistant to learning about new tools if they do not fit the stereotypical profile of having high Openness to Change.

Choosing instructional activities to match the stereotypical profile requires reflection and continuous improvement. How is a librarian to know if he or she is reaching engineering and science students? Assessment is always important in library instruction, and particularly when one is attempting to design instructional activities that appeal to most students. Assessment items should address specific elements of the instruction, such as asking students to indicate their degree of agreement or disagreement with statements:

The instructor created a welcoming class climate.
The Think-Pair-Share activity involved me in the class.
I enjoyed learning about the new tools that the librarian presented.

Feedback from assessments can help the librarian know if the elements he or she is introducing in instruction are actually engaging students.

The effectiveness of incorporating new elements in instruction depends partly on the librarian's level of comfort with them. To take just one example, how is the librarian to create a caring class climate to support students who may be stressed or low on Emotional Stability, if the librarian is relatively low on Warmth and Emotional Stability, too? The librarian will need to experiment with instructional behaviors that seem feasible to him or her, such as smiling more if he or she does not normally do that, avoiding correcting students who volunteer to answer questions, using open nonverbal communication (for example, not crossing his or her arms), and creating experiences at the beginning of class that connect the material to students' own interests and concerns. Maintaining a continuing flow of interaction with students throughout the class will also contribute to students' perceptions that the librarian cares. The librarian can do this through using total participation techniques and asking students if the material makes sense to them or seems useful. The more effort the librarian puts into instructional design and delivery, the more likely he or she will be to connect with students. Also, putting extra effort into instruction can enhance librarians' comfort with teaching.

5.3 ADAPTING TO INFORMALLY ASSESSED STUDENT CHARACTERISTICS

The librarian is usually faced with teaching students whom he or she has not previously met. How does the librarian ascertain students' characteristics and adapt to these? One way is by forming informal impressions of students' personality traits and perhaps learning preferences based on brief interactions with them. It is typical for people to make inferences about others' characteristics based on "thin slices" of behavior, which Ambady, Bernieri, and Richeson (2000) define as interactions or observations lasting less that 5 minutes. As they point out, some social inferences are made in the matter of seconds. The accuracy of such inferences can depend on such factors as observability of the trait, whether the trait taps into emotion or affect, and the channel of communication. For example, observable traits such as Extraversion are easier to assess from thin slices of behavior than neuroticism. Reliability of inferences can also vary depending on the medium in which the behavior was available.[15]

The responses of the survey I gave science and engineering librarians showed that it was not uncommon to adjust to the (inferred) personality characteristics and learning preferences of scientists and engineers when communicating with them. Librarians were readily able to form impressions about whether individuals they knew were Introverted or Extraverted, Lively or serious, and Open or resistant to change, for example.

Some traits are easier to observe in brief interactions than others, of course. It would be difficult to tell if an individual was Self-Reliant without knowing them fairly well, for instance. In addition, interactions with students in classroom settings offer only very small samples of behavior. Nevertheless, it is sometimes easy to tell who the Extraverts are, since they may strike up a conversation with the instructor, as well as volunteer in class. Making a connection with these Extraverted students could be as simple as engaging them in conversation. Some other traits could be informally assessed by asking students questions such as:

Do you feel stressed out when finding technical information? The answer to this question might point to anxiety and possibly low Emotional Stability.

Do you prefer to learn things by trying them out? The answer to this question could point to an active learning preference.

---

[15]Consult the original article for Ambady et al.'s findings on the several factors that influence reliability and accuracy of social judgments of personality traits.

Do you prefer to learn things by reading about them? The answer to this question could point to a reflective learning preference.

Do you like to learn about new search tools, or stick with familiar ones? The answer to this question might point to students' level of Openness to Experience or Openness to Change.

Clickers would be a good tool to assess the diversity of students' answers to these questions, but one could also ask students to answer a Qualtrics or Doodle poll on their smartphones or computers, or use a smartphone-based real-time audience response system. The poll could also be sent to students before the class or put on the course management site. I recommend that the poll be anonymous to make anxious students more comfortable and ready to disclose information about themselves.

Informal assessments of personality traits and learning style preferences, either through observations of behavior or polls, give the librarian working knowledge of student characteristics that may affect learning. While the librarian would not be able to match anonymous poll responses to individual students, he or she could at least be aware how characteristics vary among students in the class.

The idea of flexibly adapting teaching to class characteristics is described in Adaptive Teaching Theory (Randi & Corno, 2005). Randi and Corno found that teachers tend to form informal assessments of students (usually based on observation, since school and teachers have access to students for many class periods). They then flexibly adjust their teaching to groups of students and develop aptitudes in these groups. Examples of groups that teachers might naturally observe in their classes are higher ability students, lower ability students, quiet students, and anxious students. While the librarian usually does not have the luxury of observing students over many class periods—unless they are instructors of credit-bearing courses—they can conduct the kinds of informal assessments described above.

The librarian needs to be flexible and prepared to adapt to characteristics of students in the class. For example, if some students are anxious about finding technical information, the librarian could ask them to write down questions they have about the process. When I had the opportunity to teach two sessions of a civil engineering technical writing class, I asked students to write down questions they had about finding technical information at the end of the first class. Then at the beginning of the second class, I created a Powerpoint addressing these questions. On other occasions I have asked students to write down questions or comments at the end of class and to provide their email address if they want a response.

Now that the three kinds of matching have been defined, I will now discuss a few studies supporting matching instructional features to students' personality characteristics or Kolb learning styles. Studies that did not support matching instructional methods to student personality traits or learning styles will be reviewed in the next chapter.

5.4 STUDIES SUPPORTING MATCHING TO PERSONALITY CHARACTERISTICS

One feature that appears to be congruous with students' personality traits is their preference for lecturer personality traits. Chamorro-Premuzic, Furnham, Christopher, Garwood, and Martin (2008) found that students' preference for lecturer traits was correlated with their own Big Five personality traits:

> Students' neuroticism was significantly positively correlated with preference for agreeable lecturers, whilst students' extraversion correlated negatively with preference for neurotic, and positively with preference for extraverted lecturers. On the other hand, open students tended to dislike both neurotic and agreeable lecturers, preferring those high on openness. Agreeableness in students correlated positively with preference for open, agreeable, and conscientious lecturers, whereas conscientious students disliked neurotic, but liked extraverted and conscientious lecturers.

Thus, scientists, who are high on Openness, should prefer lecturers high in Openness who are not Neurotic or too Agreeable. Engineering and science students who are Introverted should prefer Introverted lecturers. Engineering and science students who are Less Conscientious should prefer Introverted and less Conscientious lecturers. Thus, in general, engineering and science students should prefer lecturers with rather similar traits to themselves. Librarians' own typical Introversion and lower Conscientiousness, as well as high Openness, should match well with these students' traits. These assertions assume the "stereotypical profile" matching approach discussed above. Obviously not all students will like the same kinds of personality traits in lecturers since their own personality traits will differ.

Not surprisingly, another area of match between student personality traits and preference for instructional features was in group work experience. Introverts enjoyed group work less, felt less valued, and were less likely to think that group members trusted each other, than Extraverts did in a sample of psychology students in the United Kingdom. (Walker, 2007). On the other hand, academic achievement in the class was not significantly different between Introverts and Extraverts. An implication of this finding is that Introverted science and engineering students will enjoy group work less than their Extraverted colleagues. Still, some types of group work, such as Think-Pair-Share, may be more palatable to Introverts than other kinds of collaborative learning activities.

Another study in the United Kingdom found that medical students' personality characteristics were associated with preferences for teaching methods. "Emotionally stable, open, and agreeable students tended to prefer lab classes, small group tutorials, and clinical training, while conscientious students tended to prefer clinical training and discussion groups (which were also highly rated by open students). Introverts were more likely to prefer independent study than were their extravert counterparts" (Chamorro-Premuzic, Furnham, & Lewis, 2007). Interestingly, none of the personality traits were associated with preferring lectures. While the authors point out that these results would not necessarily generalize to other disciplines than medical education, I believe that the study provides support for the idea that it might be good to match particular teaching modalities to student personality characteristics. Of course, more empirical studies like this one are needed to ascertain which teaching modalities could be beneficially matched to particular student personality characteristics, since it may not always be easy to see the ways that different teaching methods are congruous with personality traits.

5.5 STUDIES SUPPORTING MATCHING TO KOLB LEARNING STYLES

While there have been criticisms of matching instructional methods to learning styles, and these will be discussed in the next chapter, some studies have given evidence that congruence between instructional features and learning style characteristics can at times be beneficial. Hayes and Allinson (1996) reviewed five studies from the 1970s and 1980s that "provided some measure of support for the hypothesis that matching learning style and learning activity would improve learning achievement." They also concluded from reviewing other studies that matching the learning styles of trainers and trainees would positively influence the trainee's attitudes towards the trainer, but that there was "no clear evidence of any positive effect of a match on learning performance."

Kolb and Kolb (2013) found that different learning style types enjoy different learning activities, or even "learning spaces," which the authors view not just as the physical classroom environment, but as incorporating "physical, cultural, institutional, social, and psychological aspects." To give just one example, individuals with the Initiating learning style prefer dynamic learning spaces where they can get things done and try out things. They like their teachers to be coaches or mentors.

The three most common Kolb learning style types for Engineering and Science and Mathematics students are Analyzing, Thinking, and Deciding, which all have high Abstract Conceptualization. Analyzing types enjoy using and developing analytical and conceptual skills. They "may prefer lectures, readings, exploring analytical models, and having time to think things through," like to work alone, and like for their teachers to model their own reasoning process in lectures or individual interactions with them. Thinking types like well-structured learning situations, as well as designing and conducting experiments and manipulating data. They need time to think things through on their own and they value teachers for expertise. Individuals who favor the Deciding learning style like to "experiment with new ideas, simulations, laboratory assignments, and practical applications." They like clear standards and unambiguous evaluation procedures.

Thus people with different Kolb learning style types tend to enjoy different kinds of activities and teaching styles, and matching instruction to a learning style could involve offering learning activities and instructional characteristics that tend to be preferred by people with the style.

5.6 METHODS OF MATCHING TO INDIVIDUAL CHARACTERISTICS

How does one select instructional activities or features that match individuals' personality characteristics or learning styles? In my view, one can either select activities based on their *conceptual* alignment with individual characteristics, or choose activities that have been *empirically* shown to be preferred by individuals with different personality characteristics or learning styles. The two methods may overlap: that is, empirically proven activities may be conceptually compatible with definitions of personality traits and learning styles; and conceptually congruent activities may prompt empirical testing.

An example of a conceptually chosen activity would be offering an independent study activity designed to appeal to Self-Reliant individuals. A librarian might give students time to come up with their own criteria for evaluating a source for its usefulness to a design problem. This choice would be based on known characteristics of individuals scoring high in Self-Reliance, but would not as yet have been empirically verified. Informal assessment could determine whether the technique worked for the class as a whole, but the librarian would not be able to tell if it worked because many individuals scored high on Self-Reliance. Another reason it might work would be because of learning style since it involves Abstract Conceptualization and Active Experimentation. Or it might work because it is an Introverted activity. Or it might work for general pedagogical principles not having to do with personality or learning style exclusively. At any rate, the librarian does not know which students in the class score high on Self-Reliance and thus cannot confirm that Self-Reliance was positively correlated with liking the activity.

It might seem based on these considerations that it would not be good to select instructional activities based purely on their conceptual congruence with personality and learning style characteristics. At the same time, I believe that it is useful at least to analyze potential instructional activities through the lens of personality and learning styles. At the very least, this might give clues why a chosen instructional activity did not work in a class. In addition, knowing the characteristics of personality traits and learning styles gives the librarian ideas for experimenting with varying his or her instructional techniques. For example, a librarian who has not used Think-Pair-Shares might benefit from testing them out during a class because of their conceptual congruence with known characteristics of Introverted individuals.

Successful instructional techniques may be examined for conceptual congruence with personality and learning style descriptions. For example, consider the case study employing active learning techniques by Quigley and McKenzie (2003). The authors taught engineering technical communication classes over a number of years and their instructional methods evolved as they learned what worked and did not work with the students. They started out with a noninteractive lecture format that they felt did not engage the students adequately. In my opinion, this instructional method would appeal to Assimilative learners, but not Divergers, Convergers, and Accommodators.

Then they implemented a checklist for the students to follow in hands-on computer practice. This was viewed by some students as busy-work. I believe this activity did not work because it did not appeal to students who were high in Reasoning. It may also have been boring and overly prescriptive to any students who were high on Openness to Change and low on Rule-Consciousness or Perfectionism. It may not have appealed to students' creativity.

The authors next offered a class combining elements of lecture, class discussion, and individual hands-on practice. One minute papers were assigned to capture students' reflections about the class. In my view, this class would have appealed both to active and reflective learners, and Extraverts and Introverts. Creative students (high on Openness to Change and possibly low on Rule-Consciousness and Perfectionism) had some flexibility to construct their own searches. The class was challenging, but did not contain "trick questions." Thus it would appeal to students high in Reasoning and would accommodate any students low on Emotional Stability since there was a lot of individualized attention. Specifically, in the context of supporting less resilient or more anxious students, it is notable that the authors recommended, "Develop activities with successful outcomes that motivate rather than discourage students." The authors also recommended, "Identify your hook" (find a way to motivate students to participate). This is in alignment with the first quadrant of Kolb's learning cycle (Concrete Experience and Reflective Observation), in which a connection is made between the learning material and students' previous experience.

All in all, Quigley and McKenzie's case study shows that effective teaching can naturally accommodate different learning styles and personality characteristics, even if this was not the instructors' conscious intention at the outset. Quigley and McKenzie did design their instruction to appeal to visual and verbal learning styles, but they did not mention incorporating Kolb learning styles or personality traits.

5.7 CONCLUSION

Well-balanced instruction, tailoring instruction to the stereotypical profile, and adapting to students during the instructional moment are ways to match instruction to personality characteristics and learning styles. Some research supports providing instruction that is congruous with student traits. Choosing instructional activities that are congruous with student characteristics may be based either on conceptual definitions of personality traits and learning styles, or empirical findings. This process is a nontrivial task. The next chapter will explore reasons why in some cases it might be good *not* to match instruction with students' personality characteristics and learning styles.

REFERENCES

Ambady, N., Bernieri, F. J., & Richeson, J. A. (2000). Toward a histology of social behavior: Judgmental accuracy from thin slices of the behavioral stream. *Advances in Experimental Social Psychology, 32*, 201–271. http://dx.doi.org/10.1016/S0065-2601(00)80006-4.

Beard, C. (2010). *The experiential learning toolkit: Blending practice with concepts.* London: Kogan Page Publishers.

Chamorro-Premuzic, T., Furnham, A., Christopher, A. N., Garwood, J., & Martin, G. N. (2008). Birds of a feather: Students' preferences for lecturers' personalities as predicted by their own personality and learning approaches. *Personality and Individual Differences, 44*(4), 965–976. http://dx.doi.org/10.1016/j.paid.2007.10.032.

Chamorro-Premuzic, T., Furnham, A., & Lewis, M. (2007). Personality and approaches to learning predict preference for different teaching methods. *Learning and Individual Differences, 17*(3), 241–250. http://dx.doi.org/10.1016/j.lindif.2006.12.001.

Dabbour, K. S. (1997). Applying active learning methods to the design of library instruction for a freshman seminar. *College & Research Libraries, 58*(4), 299–308.

Hayes, J., & Allinson, C. W. (1996). The implications of learning styles for training and development: A discussion of the matching hypothesis. *British Journal of Management, 7*(1), 63–73. http://dx.doi.org/10.1111/j.1467-8551.1996.tb00106.x.

Himmele, P., & Himmele, W. (2011). *Total participation techniques: Making every student an active learner.* Alexandria, VA: ASCD.

Jussim, L. (1986). Self-fulfilling prophecies: A theoretical and integrative review. *Psychological Review, 93*(4), 429. http://dx.doi.org/10.1037/0033-295X.93.4.429.

Kolb, D. A. (2015). *Experiential learning: Experience as the source of learning and development* (2nd ed.). Upper Saddle River, NJ: Pearson Education Ltd..

Kolb, A. Y., & Kolb, D. A. (2013). *The Kolb Learning Style Inventory 4.0: A comprehensive guide to the theory, psychometrics, research on validity and educational applications.* Experience Based Learning Systems, Inc.

McCarthy, B., & McCarthy, D. (2006). *Teaching around the 4MAT® cycle: Designing instruction for diverse learners with diverse learning styles.* Thousand Oaks, CA: Corwin Press.

Nelson, M. S. (2014). Find the real need. In M. Fosmire & D. F. Radcliffe (Eds.), *Integrating information into the engineering design process* (pp. 87–100). West LaFayette, IN: Purdue University Press.

Quigley, B. D., & McKenzie, J. (2003). Connecting engineering students with the library: A case study in active learning. *Issues in Science and Technology Librarianship, 37.*

Randi, J., & Corno, L. (2005). Teaching and learner variation. *British Journal of Educational Psychology, 2,* 47–69.

Rosati, P. (1993). Student retention from first-year engineering related to personality type. In *Paper presented at the 23rd annual conference on frontiers in education: Engineering education: Renewing America's Technology, November 6, 1993–November 9, 1993, Washington, DC.* http://dx.doi.org/10.1109/FIE.1993.405572.

Tewell, E. C. (2014). What stand-up comedians teach us about library instruction four lessons for the classroom. *College & Research Libraries News, 75*(1), 28–30.

Tomlinson, C. A. (2014). *Differentiated classroom: Responding to the needs of all learners.* Alexandria, VA: ASCD.

Walker, A. (2007). Group work in higher education: Are introverted students disadvantaged? *Psychology Learning & Teaching, 6*(1), 20–25. http://dx.doi.org/10.2304/plat.2007.6.1.20.

CHAPTER 6

Reasons for *Not* Matching Instruction to Individual Differences

6.1 EVIDENCE AGAINST EFFECTIVENESS OF TEACHING TO LEARNING STYLES

Perhaps one of the most troubling concerns about the prospect of adapting teaching to learning styles is the lack of evidence that tailoring instruction to learning styles improves student performance. Pashler, McDaniel, Rohrer, and Bjork made the case that a particular kind of evidence is necessary to show the usefulness of learning styles (2008).

> To provide evidence for the learning-styles hypothesis—whether it incorporates the meshing hypothesis or not—a study must satisfy several criteria. First, on the basis of some measure or measures of learning style, learners must be divided into two or more groups (e.g., putative visual learners and auditory learners). Second, subjects within each learning-style group must be randomly assigned to one of at least two different learning methods (e.g., visual versus auditory presentation of some material). Third, all subjects must be given the same test of achievement (if the tests are different, no support can be provided for the learning-styles hypothesis). Fourth, the results need to show that the learning method that optimizes test performance of one learning-style group is different from the learning method that optimizes the test performance of a second learning-style group.

Pashler et al. concluded that there were no studies showing that learning styles interacted with learning method in this way to predict achievement. While Pashler et al. did not deny the existence of learning styles, they asserted that the practical significance of learning styles was not supported by the evidence.

Coffield, Moseley, Hall, and Ecclestone (2004) also cited studies questioning the effectiveness of matching Kolb learning styles to instructional methods. For example, they cite Smith, Sekar, and Townsend's statement, "For each research study supporting the principle of matching instructional style and learning style, there is a study rejecting the matching hypothesis"

Teaching to Individual Differences in Science and Engineering Librarianship
http://dx.doi.org/10.1016/B978-0-08-101881-1.00006-6

(2002, p. 411). This study found eight studies supporting matching and eight studies not supporting matching. In addition, Coffield et al. cite Mainemelis, who reported on two dissertations reviewing the evidence for matching instruction to Kolb learning styles. These dissertations, authored by Hickox and Iliff, showed mixed evidence for Experiential Learning Theory and the Learning Styles Inventory. Coffield et al. also call attention to the small sample sizes in many of the studies attempting to validate Kolb's learning styles framework.

Thus the bottom-line effectiveness on performance of matching instructional methods with Kolb learning styles has been called into question. Coffield et al. also allude to the practical difficulties of individualizing instruction, particularly in large classes with modular formats, although they report on Kolb's belief that information technology may "provide the breakthrough, together with a shift in the teacher's role from 'dispenser of information to coach or manager of the learning process'" (1984, p. 202).

I contend that even if matching instructional methods to Kolb learning styles does not have a quantitative effect on performance, this fact does not rule out other kinds of effects. For example, matching instructional methods to learning styles may contribute to satisfaction with the instruction or enjoyment of the learning process.

6.2 CHALLENGING THE STUDENT TO BECOME MORE WELL-ROUNDED

Kolb (2015) states that it is important to consider integrative objectives for students—i.e., "objectives for growth and creativity"—in addition to objectives related to course content and developing the predominant learning style of the discipline.

> In making students more 'well-rounded,' the aim is to develop the weaknesses in the students' learning style to stimulate growth in their ability to learn from a variety of learning perspectives. Here the goal is something more than making students' learning styles adaptive for their particular career entry job. The aim is to make the student self-renewing and self-directed; to focus on integrative development where the person is highly developed in each of the four learning modes; active, reflective, abstract, and concrete. Here the student is taught to experience the tension and conflict among these orientations, for it is from the resolution of these tensions that creativity springs.

Kolb makes the point that tension between Divergence and Convergence can contribute to creativity in physics, which has Convergence as its primary learning style. Intuition and flexibility are important to scientific innovations, and these characteristics are typically found in Divergers. He surmises that younger physicists may at times be more creative than older ones because they have not yet fully developed a Convergent style.

Engineering and science educators who try to instill professional and soft skills in their students at times must encourage them to use personality traits and learning modes that they may not find comfortable. For example, teaching engineering and science students about teamwork may challenge these typically introverted learners to display more Extraverted and Agreeable behaviors. Similarly, writing assignments may encourage students with active learning modes to engage in reflection.

Information literacy skills similarly require students to be reflective as well as active. Information literacy is not just about "library logistics" or learning the mechanics of searching databases; it also requires students to reflect critically on how information was produced and how it is part of a larger scholarly conversation. In a later chapter, I enumerate the personality traits that seem to be consonant with the ACRL Information Literacy Framework for Higher Education, comparing and contrasting these with the characteristics that seem to be congruous with the ABET Criterion 3 engineering standard.

Besides developing professional and information literacy skills, students in engineering and the science need to be able to solve real-world problems that require using a variety of learning styles and personality traits. As I mentioned in a previous chapter, the stages of engineering design seem to involve all parts of the Kolb learning cycle. It is likely that when engineering and science students begin working in organizations, they also will have to interact with a variety of co-workers and customers who may not fit their disciplinary norm in respect to personality traits or learning styles.

6.3 NONMATCHING AS AN IMPETUS TO IMPROVE TEACHING

The sense that he or she has not adequately connected with engineering and science students may cause librarians to reflect on ways to improve their teaching. While not all failures to connect are due to differences between librarians and students in personality traits or learning styles,[16] there are some potential mismatches. Librarians typically differ from these students on Sensitivity, with librarians being more sensitive than the norm population

---

[16]For example, librarians as a group share Introversion and low Emotional Stability with many engineering and science students, and these traits can lead to failures to connect.

and engineers being more utilitarian than the norm. Other possible mismatches may occur when some librarians have a Diverging instead of a Converging learning style (which is more typical of engineers), and when some librarians are more reflective than those engineering and science students who tend to be more active.

Being aware of engineering students' typically low scores on Sensitivity can prompt librarians to focus on providing practical, logical examples rather than communicating humanistic values about information. Whereas many librarians may have an aesthetic or humanistic bent, many engineering students do not share this characteristic. Librarians may want to explain the objective real world applicability of any information they are teaching.

Some librarians may also have a Diverging learning style, which is diametrically opposed to the converging style that is typical of many engineering students. Divergers prefer Concrete Experience and Reflective Observation while Convergers prefer Abstract Conceptualization and Active Experimentation. Divergers tend to be imaginative and people-oriented, whereas Convergers are more interested in technical matters. While not all librarians are Divergers, and not all engineering and science students are Convergers, one could see this as creating a mismatch in some cases.

In addition, some librarians, whether Divergers or Assimilators, may be more reflective than those students who have active learning styles. On a personal note, my awareness that I have a reflective learning style (Assimilation) led me to make my instruction more active. Instead of just lecturing, as I used to do, I began incorporating interactive exercises in my classes. The results of the survey reported in a later chapter showed that many librarians incorporate active learning in their instruction. While active learning experiences and interaction are probably important for all kinds of students, regardless of their natural learning style, it may not occur to very reflective librarians to provide opportunities for active learning.

Experiences when classes did not go well can thus provide the impetus for improving instruction and knowing about their own personality traits and learning styles can provide librarians material for metacognitive reflecting on their teaching. Kolb and Kolb (2013, p. 29) pointed out the usefulness of their framework for metacognitive reflection.

> By using the experiential learning model, learners can better understand the learning process, themselves as learners and the appropriate use of learning strategies based on the learning task and environment. When individuals engaged in the process of learning by reflective monitoring of the learning process they are going through, they can begin to understand important aspects of learning: how they

move through each stage of the learning cycle, the way their unique learning style fits with how they are being taught, and the learning demands of what is being taught. This comparison results in strategies for action that can be applied in their ongoing learning process.

Similarly, awareness of one's personality traits can be useful for metacognition about teaching. For example, the awareness that I am highly introverted allowed me to realize ways in which this could keep me from connecting with students and prompted me to incorporate more interaction in my classes.

6.4 SUBJECT MATTER CHARACTERISTICS

Matching instruction to learning styles or personality may not be appropriate when content considerations strongly influence how the subject matter needs to be taught. In some cases it may not be beneficial to include activities for learning styles that are quite different from the subject matter. Kolb (2015) makes the point that considering subject matter is essential for deciding what approach to take with teaching students. For example, he says that teaching empathic listening requires a different approach from teaching statistics. Similarly, Peterson, Carne, and Freear studied teacher trainees' attitudes towards styles (including learning styles) and quoted a mathematics teacher's objection to tailoring instruction to style. The mathematics teacher said that the subject matter was "very rigid and logical in structure, so there will always tend to be bias towards the analytical end of the spectrum" (2015). In my view, it is helpful to analyze the subject matter to see if it naturally lends itself to being taught with a variety of instructional methods to appeal to different learning styles and personality characteristics. The librarian may ask himself or herself the following guiding questions in analyzing subject matter.

6.5 GUIDING QUESTIONS ABOUT MATCHING TO SUBJECT MATTER

6.5.1 Learning Styles

1. Does the subject matter contain abstract or concrete content? (Or both.)
    This question gets at the Abstract Conceptualization and Concrete Experience dimensions of Kolb's learning styles framework. An example of highly abstract subject matter is mathematics, and highly concrete is studio art.

2. Does the subject matter require learning hands-on techniques?

This gets at the Active Experimentation aspect of the Kolb framework. An example of the kind of subject matter that requires learning hand-on laboratory techniques is chemistry.

3. Does the subject matter lend itself to thoughtful reflection?

This gets at the Reflective Observation dimension of Kolb's system. An example of subject matter that would require students to engage in reflection is history. More active courses may not exclude the need for reflection, as well, however. For example, Cowan describes numerous examples of the effective use of reflection in engineering (2006).

6.5.2 Personality

1. Does the subject matter lend itself to Introverted or Extraverted activities? (Or both.)

For example, a speech communication class would require students to demonstrate some degree of Extraverted behaviors. On the other hand, a cataloging class in a library science program would require students to take part in activities requiring focused, solitary concentration (Introversion).

2. Does the subject matter require students to demonstrate a high degree of emotional resilience?

This question gets at the trait of Emotional Stability. One might imagine that internships in emergency medicine would require the students to demonstrate high degrees of Emotional Stability.

3. Does the subject matter stimulate continuous learning of new information?

While arguably any subject matter that is new will involve learning new information, I believe that some fields require students to demonstrate Openness to Change more than others. Science and engineering subject matter, with their constantly changing developments in knowledge, would seem to require a high degree of Openness to Change.

4. Does the subject matter require students to think logically and analytically, or more intuitively and subjectively? Does the subject matter deal with objective, practical, real-world concerns? Or does it have more of a humanistic, aesthetic focus?

Subject matter that requires logical thinking requires a high degree of tough-minded behavior and low Sensitivity. An example would be mathematics. Subject matter requiring a lower degree of Tough-Mindedness might include art. One would use real-world examples and practical case studies when teaching subject matter congruous with having low Sensitivity. One would use more of a humanities approach when teaching topics requiring students to demonstrate higher Sensitivity.

This checklist is not exhaustive; it merely shows that different forms of knowledge may best be taught with different approaches. Just as disciplines tend to attract individuals with congruent learning styles and personality traits, instructional methods may need to be congruous with the subject matter, as well. Trying to match instruction to all learning styles or personality characteristics may water down what is essential about the subject matter.

The question arises, does science and engineering information literacy need to be taught in a particular way due to its subject matter, or can it be adapted to a variety of individuals with different characteristics in a class? To answer this question, I now apply the preceding checklist to STEM information literacy subject matter.

Abstract vs concrete content:

Some information literacy content is conceptual, such as the concepts of search operators, lifelong learning, and plagiarism, while some knowledge is more concrete. Examples of concrete information would be the names and looks of databases, library locations, and particular search features of individual resources.

Hands-on activities:

Practice using databases or completion of checklists are examples of hands-on (active) learning activities.

Reflection:

Minute papers and absorbing information from lectures give students the chance to engage in Reflective Observation.

Introversion/Extraversion:

Listening to a lecture is an Introverted activity. Class discussion is more Extraverted.

Emotional Resilience:

Typically, I do not think information literacy classes would be very stressful for students since they are usually not graded and since the librarian is there to help students.

Continuous Learning:

Information literacy classes in STEM typically present novel information that can best be taught in a way that appeals to individuals high in Openness to Change. Since lifelong learning is so important for both scientists and engineers, information literacy classes should emphasize this value.

Logic and Analytical Thinking:

Some aspects of STEM information literacy can be taught in a logical way. For example, one could give a checklist of criteria for evaluating sources that would allow students to assess rationally the quality of information. On the other hand, the librarian may also want to mention to students that sometimes searching for information is a trial-and-error, serendipitous process.

Objective, Practical, Real-World Concerns vs Humanistic Focus:

Even if the librarian himself or herself has high scores on Sensitivity, the content of information literacy classes does not have to require an aesthetic/humanistic focus. Information literacy can be seen as a primarily pragmatic activity, even though there are certainly philosophical values embedded in the process of using information.

Based on this analysis, it seems to me that STEM information literacy instruction, by virtue of its content, needs to include activities that foster, or appeal to, high Openness to Change. However, information literacy learning activities could fall on either pole of several other personality trait and learning style dimensions, For instance, information literacy does not have to include mostly Introverted or mostly Extraverted activities by virtue of its subject matter.

6.6 WHEN TO MATCH INSTRUCTION TO INDIVIDUAL DIFFERENCES, AND WHEN NOT TO

In addition to analyzing whether the content of information literacy instruction necessitates using certain teaching approaches, the librarian can analyze when it is appropriate to personalize instruction based on this and the preceding chapter.

First, the librarian can consider whether to offer "well-balanced instruction," matching many personality traits and learning style characteristics of students in a class. Decision criteria include the following:

1. Is it practical to offer a variety of techniques?
2. Is offering a variety of techniques going to offer any benefits?

Practical constraints include class time, number of students, familiarity with alternative instructional techniques, and STEM faculty buy-in. There is a limit to the number of techniques that the librarian can use if he or she only has 50 minutes to meet with students. He or she may have to be selective about personalization activities, for example, focusing only on the Introversion/Extraversion personality dimension and the active/reflective learning style dimension.

In addition, the number of students is a factor. It will be difficult to do some total participation techniques such as Chalkboard Splash if there are more than 20 students in the room. Similarly, offering hands–on practice may be more feasible with small class sizes and "rovers" to provide assistance.

Third, the librarian may not know how to vary instructional techniques. Many librarians have never taken a course in instruction and have had to learn on the job and through continuing education opportunities or through observation of colleagues. However, recognizing areas of mismatch either between their own characteristics and students' (or the content's characteristics) may encourage them to undertake this kind of self-education.

Fourth, engineering and science teaching faculty may not be open to a great deal of experimentation in instructional methods, as well. Engineering professors, for example, may focus on the need to fulfill ABET lifelong learning requirements, and they may be uninterested in librarians' taking the time to offer a variety of instructional techniques.

The other decision criterion, i.e., whether well-balanced instruction is going to offer any benefits, is not easy to assess, since the librarian is obviously not conducting controlled experiments measuring "crossover interactions" between student characteristics and instructional treatments (Pashler et al., 2008). At the same time, the arguments voiced in the preceding chapter for providing a variety of instructional methods apply.

As well as deciding whether to offer well-balanced instruction, the librarian can decide whether to tailor instruction to the stereotypical profile of science and engineering students. The following are a few decision criteria to use.

1. Is it likely that students in general share certain personality characteristics or learning styles?
2. Is the subject matter congruous with these personality characteristics and learning styles as well?
3. Is it necessary to make the students more well rounded in this instance, stretching them to exhibit behaviors outside of the stereotypical profile?

Using the stereotypical profile approach might not be appropriate in an introductory science class in which there are many nonmajors. Students from other majors would not necessarily be expected to exhibit the same personality and learning style characteristics as students attracted to majoring in the sciences or engineering. The librarian should also remember that some students in lower level classes may switch their major from the sciences or engineering. The librarian also needs to remember that despite person-environment fit and the accentuation of learning styles within a discipline, there will still be heterogeneity in personality characteristics and learning styles within a major.

A second thing to consider is whether the information literacy subject matter is congruous with the stereotypical profile of students in science or engineering. For example, searching may at times be a trial-and-error process that does not appeal to highly logical, tough-minded individuals who are low on Sensitivity. It might be important to show students the iterative, sometimes serendipitous nature of the information retrieval process, even if the process does not appeal to them personally. Other characteristics of the information literacy subject matter, may align well with personality traits and learning styles of engineering and science students, however. For example, I have mentioned that information literacy content is congruous with high Openness to Change since it emphasizes lifelong learning and the continuous acquisition of new knowledge. High Openness to Change is found in the profiles of engineers, scientists, and librarians.

Third, in some instances it may be important to challenge students to exhibit behaviors different from the stereotypical profile. For example, engineering design students who are learning how to gather information from customers may have to engage in Extraverted behaviors such as interviewing clients. Similarly, students who are used to a more active learning style may have to stretch to become more reflective when analyzing whether information is high quality, technical information. Growth is possible when students are challenged to develop new skills that may not come naturally to them.

When designing instruction to fit the stereotypical profile, the librarian should consider all of these factors and not force all aspects of the instruction to be congruous with characteristics of typical engineering or science students. I think the stereotypical profile can give the librarian some ideas of ways in which to engage students; however, and to form a connection with them during the often too brief periods of class time with them.

When deciding whether to adapt to individual differences during the instructional moment, the librarian may want to consider these factors:

1. Is adaptation likely to make a difference in the student's engagement or comprehension of material?
2. Are the characteristics that the librarian is considering adapting to fairly easy to ascertain?
3. Is the adaptation appropriate for teaching the material?

The first factor concerns the likely efficacy of making an adaptation to the individual during the instructional moment. Being observant of personality characteristics such as Introversion or Extraversion or low emotional stability, and adapting to these traits, can make a difference in the student's comfort and engagement, my experience has shown. For example, when a class is primarily composed of Introverts, it makes sense to offer opportunities for extraverts to contribute, as well. In classes I have taught, Extraverted students have struck up conversations before or after class, asked questions during class, or been the first to volunteer in class discussion. If there were no opportunities for interaction, these students might have been less engaged. Similarly, when I have encountered stressed out students (possibly low on Emotional Stability), I have always thought it was important to reassure them at the outset that we would be able to find the information they needed.

The second factor concerns the practicality of attempting to surmise student personality or learning style characteristics. Given that the librarian often has only a very small sample of a student's behavior to observe, how is he or she to infer characteristics correctly? Some behaviors stand out (Extraversion, Dominance, Social Boldness) while others are less easy to ascertain (Neuroticism, Vigilance, Self-Reliance). For the sake of practicality, the librarian can choose to adapt his or her interaction only when the behavior is extreme or obvious. For example, if a seemingly highly Tough-Minded engineering student is carefully critiquing search results, the librarian can logically explain why the results were the way they were, without assuming the student is being disagreeable. Similarly, the librarian can adapt to knowledge of his or her own high Sensitivity by making examples more logical, objective, and practical.

Last, the librarian may want to consider whether adapting to a student's characteristics is appropriate for teaching the subject matter. Is time available to respond in class to an individual's concern, or might the librarian want to encourage the student to speak with him or her after class, for example? While adapting to individuals' characteristics is a natural part of one-on-one interaction, and the survey showed that librarians frequently adapted to people when communicating with them, it may not be as easy to do this effectively in group instruction settings when time is limited.

6.7 CONCLUSION

This chapter and the last have given some considerations about why at times it might be good to match instructional methods with personality characteristics and learning styles, and reasons why at times why it might be good *not* to match instruction to these characteristics. I next turn to results of a survey of STEM librarians that I conducted concerning their attitudes towards personalizing instruction and communication to personality traits and learning styles.

REFERENCES

Coffield, F., Moseley, D., Hall, E., & Ecclestone, K. (2004). *Learning styles and pedagogy in post 16 learning: A systematic and critical review.* London: The Learning and Skills Research Centre.

Cowan, J. (2006). *On becoming an innovative university teacher: Reflection in action* (2nd ed.). New York, NY: Society for Research into Higher education & Open University Press.

Kolb, D. (1984). *Experiential education: Experience as the source of learning and development.* Englewood Cliffs, NJ: Prentice Hall.

Kolb, D. A. (2015). *Experiential learning: Experience as the source of learning and development* (2nd ed.). Upper Saddle River, NJ: Pearson Education Ltd.

Kolb, A. Y., & Kolb, D. A. (2013). *The Kolb Learning Style Inventory 4.0: A comprehensive guide to the theory, psychometrics, research on validity and educational applications.* Experience Based Learning Systems, Inc.

Pashler, H., McDaniel, M., Rohrer, D., & Bjork, R. (2008). Learning styles concepts and evidence. *Psychological Science in the Public Interest, 9*(3), 105–119. http://dx.doi.org/10.1111/j.1539-6053.2009.01038.x.

Peterson, E. R., Carne, S. S., & Freear, S. J. (2015). Teaching secondary teachers about style: Should we do it? In S. Rayner & E. Cools (Eds.), *Style differences in cognition, learning, and management: Theory, research, and practice.* New York: Routledge.

Smith, W., Sekar, S., & Townsend, K. (2002). The impact of surface and reflective teaching and learning on student academic success. *Paper presented at the learning styles: Reliability and validity: Proceedings of the 7th annual European learning styles information network conference, 26–28 June, Ghent.*

CHAPTER 7

Results of Survey

Fig. 7.1 presents the questions of the survey.

7.1 RESULTS: ATTITUDES TOWARDS PERSONALIZATION

Thirty-seven librarians took the survey. Nineteen respondents indicated that they consider personality characteristics at least to some extent when planning instruction to scientists and engineers. Twelve said they did not consider personality characteristics when planning instruction for scientists and engineers, and six respondents left this question blank. Twenty-four librarians said they adjusted to scientists' and engineers' personality characteristics when communicating with them. Seven librarians indicated that they did not adjust to individual scientists' and engineers' personality characteristics when communicating with them, and six respondents left this question blank.

Sixteen librarians said they considered learning preferences when planning instruction for scientists and engineers. Nine respondents stated that they did not consider learning preferences when planning instruction to scientists and engineers. Twelve left this question unanswered. Thirteen respondents said they considered learning preferences when communicating with scientists and engineers. Eleven librarians said they did not adjust to individual scientists' and engineers' learning preferences when communicating with them, and 13 librarians did not answer this question. Thus there were many respondents who did not consider personality traits and/or learning preferences when planning instruction, and many who did not adjust to individual scientists' or engineers' personality traits and/or learning preferences when communicating with them. Before turning to responses that favored personalization of instruction and communication either to personality traits or learning preferences, I will summarize the reasons respondents provided that were unfavorable towards personalizing instruction or communication to these characteristics.

Teaching to Individual Differences in Science and Engineering Librarianship
http://dx.doi.org/10.1016/B978-0-08-101881-1.00007-8

7.1.1 Unfavorable Responses to Personalization

Reasons for not considering personality characteristics in planning instruction for scientists and engineers included the following:

> Not really. I usually try to get a feel for the class as a whole when I'm in it rather than focusing on individual characteristics.

> No. Maybe subconsciously I do, but this is not something I have ever put conscious thought into.

> Not really, I think more about what they need to do and their mindset and prior preparation rather than their personalities.

> Do not consider these for the few classes I co-teach with engineering faculty.

The first statement above seems to reflect the respondent's choice to incorporate class characteristics in instructional planning, rather than individual characteristics, such as personality. One might assume; however, that "a feel for the class as a whole" could be affected by the personalities

---

Do you provide library instruction to science and/or engineering students or faculty? Check all that apply.

- ○ Scientists
- ○ Engineers
- ○ None of the above

How long have you been a librarian?

- ○ Less than 2 years
- ○ 2–5 years
- ○ more than 5 years–10 years
- ○ more than 10 years–20 years
- ○ more than 20 years

Personality Characteristics

For the following 10 questions, please give your perceptions of the personality characteristics of yourself, scientists, and engineers. Scientists and engineers include science and engineering faculty and students.

When you rate the personality characteristics of scientists and engineers, consider typical scientists or engineers.

Fig. 7.1 Questions in the survey.

[This section contained descriptions of ten personality traits. Respondents were asked to rate themselves, scientists, and engineers on the traits.]

Do you consider any of the preceding personality characteristics *when planning your instruction* to scientists or engineers? Please explain and give examples.

Do you adjust to individual scientists' or engineers' personality characteristics *when communicating with them*? Please explain and give examples.

Learning Preferences
For the next section give your perceptions of the learning preferences of yourself, scientists, and engineers.

[This section contained descriptions of four learning preferences based on Kolb's learning style dimensions. Respondents were asked to rate themselves, scientists, and engineers on the learning preferences.]

Do you consider learning preferences such as those above *when planning instruction* for scientists and engineers? Please explain and give examples.

Do you adjust to individual scientists' and engineers' learning preferences *when communicating with them*? Please explain and give examples.

Do you think it is sometimes important to match instruction to an individual's or group's personality characteristics or learning preferences? Please explain and give examples.

Do you think it is sometimes important *not* to match instruction to an individual's or group's personality characteristics or learning preferences? Please explain and give examples.

Fig. 7.1, Cont'd

of individuals in the class. For example, if most of the individuals were Introverted, then the overall feel for the class would be that students are Introverted. The third statement reflects the respondent's focus on other characteristics than personality, prior preparation and mindset, which could affect the content the librarian would choose and motivational techniques used.

The following are reasons for "no" responses for the question about adjusting to the personality characteristics of scientists and engineers when communicating with them:

Nah. I was a scientist and am married to a scientist. I don't make any adjustments.

Not, really. but I'm trained as a scientist (PhD in geophysics) so I might communicate like a scientist/engineer without thinking about it. I do tend to write emails very differently than my humanist colleagues.

Both of these respondents seem to acknowledge that their scientific background might help them to communicate with other presumably similar scientists and engineers.

Reasons for "no" responses to considering learning preferences in planning instruction for scientists and engineers included the following:

I don't think I've planned instruction for specifically that type of audience in mind. I think I plan for the level of student and learner, rather than for the discipline. Of course the examples are (usually) discipline-specific, but the type of instruction isn't, usually. I try to: / - have lots of visuals and demos, and try to give students access to computers so that they can follow along / - give concrete examples (students seem to like that) / - give practice time / So I think that covers learning by doing and watching. //

No. I try to give every class hands-on experience related to a project they are working on.

No. There is NO EVIDENCE that learning preference has ANY influence on how much somebody learns, regardless of the way the subject is presented to them. Just because you enjoy learning by doing, doesn't mean you won't learn by watching or thinking. I don't especially care if students enjoy my instruction; I care that they learn what I wanted them to learn. And students are notoriously bad at estimating how much they've learned. A student saying they liked an instruction session means nothing; they easily could have absorbed none of the information.
I have never thought to do so, no.

I never gave that much thought to it before. I consider more learning styles than personality traits.

The first two responses indicate that the librarians employ effective instructional methods, regardless of learning styles (hands–on instruction, visuals, concrete examples, etc.) The hands–on instructional approach was employed by several respondents, as will be discussed below. The third response indicates the same attitude that critics of learning styles have towards Kolb's learning styles framework (Coffield, Moseley, Hall, & Ecclestone, 2004).

The reasons for "no" answers to adjusting to engineers' and scientists' learning styles when communicating with them included the following:

I don't think so - I just try to be as clear as possible, including screenshots where I need to provide instructions.

I cannot say that I have done this intentionally. I tend not to think about how scientists and engineers learn when I communicate with them. I'm more focused on their preferences for communication.

Not as much, largely because I tend to be communicating rather straightforward information when communicating to engineering faculty or students outside of class. Occasionally when I'm meeting with a student one-on-one, and can reasonably quickly pick up on how that student is most comfortable learning (which isn't very often), then I'll try to adapt to that style or preference.

In the first answer, the respondent seems to focus on providing an effective communication style, regardless of learning preferences. In the second, the librarian distinguishes between communication preferences and learning preferences, saying he or she is more focused on the former. In the last answer, the respondent implies that there is no need to adjust to learning styles when communicating rather straightforward information.

When asked whether they thought it was sometimes important to match instruction to personality characteristics or learning styles, the following reasons for negative or partially negative answers were given:

No because the logistics of this would be a nightmare, especially since all classes I teach are one shot sessions.

No. Again, there is NO EVIDENCE that this has any effect.

Depends. If it is one-on-one instruction yes—if it is classroom instruction it is hard to adjust for everyone's personality.

I don't think you can easily plan for group personality characteristics. I have observed that individual classes will have a unique personality all their own. It's like a group dynamic takes over; the same students can be in a different class and they behave in a different fashion. / / I do think we need to be aware of learning preferences and design our instruction accordingly.

Sure, but it's more difficult in a group, because I've never experienced a group where every person in the group had the same personality characteristics or learning preferences. There are always one or two students who are really engaged and ask a number of questions and there are always a (generally larger) group who never open their mouths. There's no instruction technique that I'm familiar with that is effective to both of those audiences.

As much as you can, although often with a class of 80 freshman, this is not possible. But I have learned that instruction isn't successful unless there is a clear need: an assigned paper or presentation has to have been given for me to go to a class. Outside of orientation for new students, I don't want to waste their time or mine.

No. recent research has shown that the learning style theories are bunk.

I do not think that this is a 100% doable option. I try to offer balance, multi-modal learning opportunities, and experiences for multiple learners in a class setting. For this to be 100% based on an individual, I would need much more information about the individual. While this is possible for all learners, is it practical? A learning environment may be designed to work for most learners. The Internet/Web is kind of like that, individuals take charge of where they go & learn.

Many of these statements mention the logistical challenges of matching instruction to personality characteristics and learning preferences when classes contain individuals who vary greatly in these respects. In particular, the librarians mention the difficulties of personalizing instruction in one-shot classes, large classes, and classes where there is no assignment or clear need for the instruction. One of the respondents also mentions he or she would not have enough information about the individual students to match instruction to everyone in the class, but that self-guided Internet instruction might make this possible. Two respondents state that there is lack of evidence for learning styles theories, similarly to Coffield et al.'s study (2004).

When asked if it is sometimes important not to match instruction to engineers' and scientists' personality characteristics and learning styles, a respondent gave the following reasons for a "no" answer:

No, I think it is always important to do if it is within your power to do so. Sometimes you just can't know the personality or learning preferences in advance.

This answer again mentions the logistical challenges of personalizing instruction to personality traits and learning styles, but implied that it is important to try to do this. All the other answers either simply answered "no" without a reason, were blank, or gave reasons why it might sometimes be good not to match instruction to personality characteristics and learning preferences.

7.1.2 Favorable Responses Towards Personalization

When asked if they considered personality characteristics in planning instruction for scientists and engineers, respondents said they tried to incorporate the following characteristics in their instruction:

1. Using illustrative or concrete examples

yes to use more illustrative examples for searching.

Any group of people varies within the group. I might pick more concrete examples for engineers, such as finding physical properties.

Training in my environment very much focuses on concrete examples - how the tools can be used by the audience rather than surveys or overviews.

I try to have all the learning possibilities clearly defined and use quality examples to support the instruction. Predicting interactions with scientists in advance is not simple. At times an individual's focus is narrow and based on abstract science concepts. I can try to find relevant language to convey meaning, but that tactic is not 100% successful.

2. Precision

I have learned to be more precise with instruction and details- less big story type of statements and more directly applicable statements.

I probably over-prepare when I work with this group because they like to know about the minutiae of resources like databases. Although I am never sorry that I overprepare!

For engineers, I focus on precise searching and finding exactly what the researcher is looking for. Generally, search terms for engineering are clear and unambiguous. Scientists often use different terms for the same idea, especially in cross-disciplinary work (e.g., geologists and hydrologists), so I make sure they understand that and use more than one term if appropriate.

3. Applicability

I have learned to be more precise with instruction and details- less big story type of statements and more directly applicable statements.

When planning instruction for scientists, I'm very conscious that the information I deliver is highly-accurate and that I qualify any statements that are more opinion-based as, 'In my opinion…' I'm also careful to select learning activities that result in a useful product such as a set of search results or a framework that they can apply to their work.

Yes. They usually want it to apply to what they are doing in the course. This is sometimes difficult when communication with the faculty members. I also have to know exactly what the project is that the course is working on.

I make sure to give a reason why we are meeting for instruction either tied to their assignment or a larger life outcome. For example, I teach PubMed in cell biology. So I open with how this will tie to their gene assignment, but also with an anecdote about medical students. Many of students want to go to professional school, so I tell them that this is a skill that they can master now and not have to worry about in grad school.

Training in my environment very much focuses on concrete examples—how the tools can be used by the audience rather than surveys or overviews.

4. Accuracy

When planning instruction for scientists, I'm very conscious that the information I deliver is highly-accurate and that I qualify any statements that are more opinion-based as, "In my opinion…" I'm also careful to select learning activities that result in a useful product such as a set of search results or a framework that they can apply to their work.

5. Consistency/tradition versus creativity/Openness to Change

Yes. The engineering culture on campus is not open to change and hard to make inroads with. Some of this is due to harsh personalities of the faculty.

Yes. I know with my science faculty and students, I can be more creative and experiment in class to try out new instructional ideas and activities with students. With engineering, on the other hand, I get the sense that faculty value consistency and are only willing to try something new if I can provide rationale for why I believe a new idea is worth trying.

I do consider reasoning and Openness to change as I describe literature databases and interface changes, etc.

6. Nonconceptual

I do consider these things, but my scientists/engineers don't want conceptual instruction in IR or BI. They just want the rote steps to getting an article.

7. Emphasis on problem-solving, numbers, or anomalies

A little bit. I try to present finding information as a problem-solving process similar to approaching other engineering problems. I try to bring more warmth and liveliness to the classroom to better engage students.

Only in a very minimal way. Engineers understand numbers, so I tend to use those when possible, like comparing the results set from a search with one set of search terms vs. the results with a better set of search terms. Engineers also understand anomalies. So I do a sample search for one class that shows a tiny results set after explaining to them that the database I'm using is the best DB out there for searching on my example topic. They seem to understand that my tiny results set size is an anomaly and are curious as to why I got the results I did (which was exactly the point in me doing that search in the first place).

8. Low Warmth and Liveliness

Yes; I work with several science departments. My patrons are more practical, less lively and emotional than students with other majors. When I plan instruction, I stay away from anything that seems "gimmicky," and we seldom play games. I tend to focus on the nuts & bolts of database searching.

9. Collaboration

I know that science students are used to working together in groups - in lab settings if not in class. So when I plan instruction for them I include group work.

10. Objectivity

> *The engineers are very objective people. When I plan a training session or elaborate a tutorial, I try to go straight to the point as much as I can.*

The themes above show that there are a variety of characteristics of scientists and engineers that librarians take into account when planning instruction for them. For the most part, the librarians try to match instruction with these characteristics, except for the characteristics of low Warmth and low Liveliness. As one respondent said, he or she tried to bring more of these qualities into the instruction:

> *A little bit. I try to present finding information as a problem-solving process similar to approaching other engineering problems. I try to bring more warmth and liveliness to the classroom to better engage students.*

In other respects, librarians tried to match instruction with the perceived precision, concreteness, pragmatism, accuracy, objectivity, and consistency or, by contrast, high Openness to Change, of scientists and engineers. In addition, librarians in some cases tried to make instruction like engineering or science work: incorporating group work, as scientists do; or emulating engineers' problem-solving process or use of numbers and anomalies.

When communicating with scientists and engineers, librarians tried to adjust to the following personality characteristics:

1. Logic

> *yes, I tend to use data when available and make arguments as logical as possible. I also emphasize usefulness and efficiency of resources.*

2. Time pressure/impatience

> *yes their concerns are different and have no patience to waste their time*

> *I try to keep everything short and to the point, regardless of audience. People are too busy as it is. Most emails I send are no more than a couple of sentences, or a paragraph at most.*

> *Of course. Short emails, clear expectations if they are supposed to do something. I use bullets or numbered lists.*

3. Interest in Applicability (pragmatism)

> *yes, I tend to use data when available and make arguments as logical as possible. I also emphasize usefulness and efficiency of resources.*

4. Introversion

> *When communicating with an individual scientist or engineering, I always adjust for their personality characteristics. For example, when I talk with*

mathematicians, who are notoriously introverted, I try to ask direct questions about the library or their research. I avoid trying to make small talk or say trivial things.

I tend to adjust, at least to a modest degree, to ANYbody's personality character-istics when communicating with them. With someone who is strong-willed, I'm more assertive back. With someone who is more timid I try to keep my mouth shut more and let them talk since for many introverts it's more difficult to open up with people.

Definitely, I know that engineering students need more persistence in drawing them out for topics in a class or in a reference interview. Molecular scientists are similar this way but natural scientists and those who deal with policy are more communicative and engaged.

5. Collaborativeness/working in teams

Since our scientists are usually working in teams, it is important to share informa-tion with the entire team when communicating. They also appreciate solutions that work for their whole lab, for example setting up a lab with iThenticate so they may collaborate regarding the papers they're authoring and improve the cited references.

6. Precision

I do try to be as specific as possible in dealing with their problems. No interpreta-tion of what words might mean—I find out precisely what they want.

Yes. When working with a scientist or engineer that is talkative and who I know is willing to explore ideas, I will take liberties to allow time for creative exploration of ideas. Whereas if I am working with a scientist or engineer who seems to value precision and efficiency I will plan in advance to be as concise as possible. I am more likely to email an engineer and set up in person meetings with scientists. The engineers I've worked with seem to not value face-to-face meetings as much as scientists.

7. Rudeness

I think I tolerate and rude behavior and/or bad communication skills than I oth-erwise would with a library colleague. For example, faculty who do not make eye contact, are abrupt or rude in their communication style.

8. Straight-forwardness

Absolutely; the communication is very straight-forward. For example, in emails, I try to get to the point of the communication and avoid irrelevant small talk.

Yes. I have a way of communicating with these groups which is usually very straight forward and to the point.

I try to simply get to the point and not be long winded.

9. Creativity

> *Yes. When working with a scientist or engineer that is talkative and who I know is willing to explore ideas, I will take liberties to allow time for creative exploration of ideas. Whereas if I am working with a scientist or engineer who seems to value precision and efficiency I will plan in advance to be as concise as possible. I am more likely to email an engineer and set up in person meetings with scientists. The engineers I've worked with seem to not value face-to-face meetings as much as scientists.*

10. Liveliness and Warmth

> *Yes, when I am one-on-one with a science student, I judge their affect to gauge how humorous/casual/friendly I should be when I'm helping them. If I'm not perceiving a lot of 'personality' (warmth), I keep the interaction very short and to-the point.*

> *I assume I have, but I am not sure. // - For the more serious personalities, I am less animated and make less jokes. I stay on task and am serious about the task at hand. / - With a more outgoing and friendly personality, I tend to smile more and make more jokes.*

11. Assertiveness

> *I tend to adjust, at least to a modest degree, to ANYbody's personality characteristics when communicating with them. With someone who is strong-willed, I'm more assertive back. With someone who is more timid I try to keep my mouth shut more and let them talk since for many introverts it's more difficult to open up with people.*

Several other librarians acknowledged that they adjusted to personality characteristics when communicating with scientists and engineers, but were not specific about the characteristics that they adjusted to:

> *I always allow them to initiate communication in the media they choose. Some students prefer email while others prefer in-person interaction. / Anecdotally, the folks who monitor our chat reference say that more of their chat reference questions are from science students, rather than from arts/social sciences/humanities students.*

> *Yes. But not based on the fact that they are scientists - this only works on an individual level. I have faculty who I know I need to communicate with only in very short emails. I have others (also scientists) who I know don't mind a longer email every now and then. I have some who I can just call on the phone. And I'm not sure these are really personality characteristics so much as they are communication preferences. Two people with very similar personalities may have very different communication preferences.*

> *yes, I think that naturally you communicate differently with different people, I follow my faculty's lead on determining the best method of communication, I also understand that they are busy and have limited time, so I stick to the point, show*

them how they can "do for themselves" and explain the reasoning behind library initiatives or projects that might affect them.

Yes, every individual has its own characteristics, so I try to adjust the tone of the session to them (when it's possible to do it).

I think that as someone who works with a wide variety of people from different disciplines that I ALWAYS adjust to a manner that will be more aligned with the person that I am working with at the time.

I do try to adjust my interactions. I can be very talkative. When communicating with individual scientists I consider my level and approach to the communication for best effect.

yes, if the class seems underwhelmed, I open it up to active learning: leave the PPT behind, and have all log on to their devices to search and ask questions designed to get them involved with answers.

The respondents in general believed it was important to adjust their communication when interacting with scientists and engineers, responding more affirmatively to this question than to any of the others in the survey. There were fewer affirmative responses to the questions about considering learning preferences when planning instruction for scientists and engineers and adjusting communication to learning preference when interacting with them. The following responses described considering learning preferences when planning instruction:

1. Learning by doing

I consider learning preferences, but assume all people want to learn by doing as a preference. So I have all students try to search for research during a class session.

I try to build in actual activities into my instruction, so they get to test out their ideas before me getting into all of the theory behind it.

Yes, my students, perhaps more than others (military academy) tend towards learning by doing. We let them do the 'driving' at the desk and they also 'do' during instruction sessions, giving examples to use, following along on their computers in the lab, and in working on their own projects with librarian help/advice

I always try to plan for an active exercise when in a class. I don't think that the "sage on the stage" benefits anyone, especially when it comes to learning about library resources and services. // Often, with a class of freshman, I try to get someone willing to come up and do some searching instead of it just being me.

I try always to do hands-on instruction for the learning by 'doing' including bringing laptops to follow along in a 100+ lecture setting.

Yes. With my science and engineering courses, I always provide a hands-on activity. It helps them draw conclusions and think critically.

Yes. I make sure there is learn-by-doing time for them, such as allowing time for them to practice what I've been teaching.

2. Learning by thinking

Yes, to a degree. I generally use exercises during a class session that require students in a class to think about an example I'm using and either supply search terminology, offer ideas about why I got lousy results from an initial search, and to think about their search topics in a different way from how they did when they walked into class a half hour earlier. I don't have much opportunity to explore the "doing" option, since most of the classes I teach in are from 40-80 students, in their classroom. That, combined with the intent of the instruction in the first place, doesn't leave much opportunity for in-class 'doing'.

3. Learning by watching and thinking

I may weigh the watching and thinking aspects of my instruction more heavily than the feeling and doing aspects. For example, I would probably not plan a discussion with a group of scientists about publication bias and focus on the moral implications for not publishing negative results. I may present it in a more factual way to demonstrate that there is publication bias and the financial structure for research that supports this bias. I am not sure I consciously make this decision to steer away from the 'feeling' aspects, but perhaps it is my own discomfort or my shared discomfort with my audience that makes me want to avoid it.

4. Learning using all four learning preferences

Yes. When planning instruction, I try to include components that stimulate learning by watching and thinking, with lots of hands on activities to allow students to "do" the work. I would not say that I have put much time into planning for allowing students time to 'feel'. Although I do make my students do a lot of personal reflective work. Such as asking students to think about their past learning experiences and to consider what they think about the library or think about their experience with scientific literature. These types of questions might evoke feelings. Though I have not intentionally 'planned' to try to get students to feel anything in particular.

5. Other/unspecified

To a degree; I try to give a lot of structure in my teaching and present information in a logical and organized fashion. I try to create opportunities for students to work on a real problem together as a class, analyze why the results turned out the way they did, and figure out alternative approaches they could take to get a better result.

yes to use more illustrative examples for searching

I try to incorporate multi-modal learning as possible in my instruction. In an online course I teach to mostly science majors all students have a reading assignment to explore the learning. They also have video-demo and simulation of the learning as an option. All students practice an aspect of the concepts/learning. And then the students demonstrate mastery by completing an interactive or written assignment.

Overall, the librarians most often focused on considering the "doing" learning preference when planning instruction for scientists and engineers. It is unclear if this was due to their pedagogical training, their own learning preferences, or their realization that engineering and science students often tend to have this learning preference.

There were fewer affirmative responses to the question about whether librarians adjusted to the learning preferences of scientists and engineers when communicating with them. One response addressed other kinds of learning preferences than the ones that the survey had asked about:

> Yes. When I get a confused reaction when explaining something verbally I also try to show them. I also send photos and video of explanations.

Other responses reiterated things said in the personality section about trying to make instruction practical, clear, and serious; and about not wasting the scientists' and engineers' time. Another response mentioned supporting communication with facts and figures.

Other responses mentioned logistical considerations by adjusting communication to learning preferences:

> Not as much, largely because I tend to be communicating rather straightforward information when communicating to engineering faculty or students outside of class. Occasionally when I'm meeting with a student one-on-one, and can reasonably quickly pick up on how that student is most comfortable learning (which isn't very often), then I'll try to adapt to that style or preference.

> I just read body language while communicating. If a person appears serious, stressed, or confused, I note those cues and try to slow down, repeat things, or check in with the individual to see if she has a question.

> I find that individuals exhibit different needs in communication. While I may predict a pattern and communicate with individuals as I know them better, I cannot make conclusions without knowledge and observation of peoples communications style. At times the communication can be brief, concise, and direct. Other times I am careful to define, spell-out, and specify more details.

Learning by doing appeared as a theme in responses to this question as in the previous one:

> Yes, I try and figure out what they are understanding best and figure out ways to teach them that way. More often than not I think they learn best by seeing it or doing it themselves, so I will walk them through it.

> I try to have members of the class/session demonstrate their searches so others can see their approach and relate more to what is going on.

Finally, another response repeated the idea that it is important to adjust to individual differences in communication, in general:

I generally adjust to individuals when communicating to people. I tend to find out what background and experiences they have and then adjust appropriately.

Several responses stated that it was sometimes important to match instruction to scientists' and engineers' personality characteristics and learning preferences. One reason was to make the instruction more engaging.

Another reason was that this contributes to good instruction:

Always, why wouldn't we as good instructors? This question is ridiculous to anyone with a teaching background or those whose main function is instruction.

yes. it's always good to meet people where they are at. just as you might adjust the level of difficulty, you can adjust your style.

Another reason was that matching stimulates learning:

Yes. Catering to characteristics and learning preferences greatly stimulates learning. So I do consider preferences. For example, I understand that most engineers are inductive learners who enjoy looking for patters and coming up with answers on their own. They would rather try database searching on their own rather than watch me show them how to do database searching. Therefore in this case I would let engineering students dive into database searching on their own with a few initial prompts or pointers and answer questions as they go. This approach has been much more effective than having engineering students first watch me demonstrate the database.

Another reason was to connect with students and not waste their time:

yes, you aren't doing your students any good if you aren't getting through to them. If your instruction session is only based on your preferences and not the ways that your students learn best then you will be doing them a disservice and wasting their time.

Another reason was to help international students by taking into account their cultural differences:

Yes, of course. For instance, when teaching international students, I think about the ways they may be used to learning, and the cultural differences that may make a difference in how they perceive the instruction.

Another response stated that it was important to match to students' preferences for group or solitary work:

Yes, it is important. Groups who like to collaborate will not learn as well in a lecture-style instruction session. They will learn better in group activities. // Likewise, individuals who are introverted and reflective may find it difficult to learn and think in a group. // Ultimately, it is best to have a variety of learning activities so that the various learning styles are addressed.

Many responses said it would be difficult to match instruction to large groups, rather than individuals; however:

Definitely for individuals, but almost never for groups. Individuals have characteristics that are usually easy to figure out quickly. Groups take time to characterize and are usually very diverse. For example, I can tell when someone isn't communicating easily verbally and is nervous, so I can bring out paper and allow them to write their question.

Another response echoed the sentiment from previous questions that learning by doing is effective with scientists and engineers:

It's hard to assess in larger groups—learn by "doing" with an unknown participant personalities or learning preferences seems to work best with scientists and engineers.

Similarly, another librarian used active learning regardless of the degree program:

when I enter a class, I ask students what specific program they are studying and then gear examples and active learning based on their specific degree or programs or classes they are currently studying.

The librarians also recognized that there were sometimes cases when it was important not to match instruction to personality characteristics and learning preferences. The following themes arose:

1. Instructor empathy with student difficulties

   Yes, sometimes it is easier to teach something you are not good at, because you can break it down to its more essential problems and understand what the difficulties people will have in understanding it, if you have them too.

2. Preparation for the real world

   Sure. Students need to learn how to deal in the real world. Not everyone is going to coddle their feelings.

3. Challenge/stretching beyond the comfort zone

   Yes! Being outside of your comfort zone is where you learn. Again, students (or faculty) enjoying the instruction is not the priority. Students learning the information is the priority.

   It is important to challenge an individual or group by focusing on the goal rather than the current preferences of a person.

Yes. Individuals need to reach beyond the limits of their characteristics & preferences. If for no other reason than to understand others and how to interact with variety.

There is nothing wrong with guiding them to think outside the box. However, when I do this, I usually lead them back to their comfort zone by the end of the class.

4. Intellectual integrity

I think it would be somewhat Intellectually fraudulent to give them *exactly* what they want vis-a-vis IR or BI. Research isn't that simple, and I'm not going to pretend it's a linear progression with discrete steps.

5. Increasing students' communication skills

I think that to be effective engineers need to learn to communicate with different groups of people and so it can be worthwhile to force students out of their comfort zone a bit.

Yes. I think it is important to expose students and faculty to new ways of thinking and learning. Doing so may include trying new methods that do not necessarily cater to one's preferable learning style. For example, I made am engineering class split into groups to do mini research assignments and then share out (as a group) with the class on what they learned. I get the sense that most engineers do not like presenting or standing in front of any group to talk. So this would not be their preferred style. However, because presenting in front of a group is an important skill for professional engineers to have, I included this experience in my lesson.

6. Logistical difficulties of matching instruction

I wouldn't consider scientists or engineers, even in a 25-person class, to be a homogeneous group. So I wouldn't want to plan an instruction session that catered exclusively to one learning style or personality type. I try to vary it so that everyone can get something out of the session.

I think for one-on-one help might be different, but when I'm teaching a class, there's no guarantee that all the students in there are scientists. I just try to create engaging session rather than worry about learning preferences

if the group has multiple characteristics and preferences, it's harder to adjust. in that case you either speak to the majority or you pick what you're more comfortable with.

Yes. If you only have 50 minutes to provide instruction, you sometimes cannot do much more than a lecture-style instruction session. // Also, the more introverted and reflective personalities may have to work in a group one day, so it's imperative for them to be forced into group work. They need to learn to work collaboratively though it may be painful at first.

7.2 PERCEPTIONS OF SCIENTISTS', ENGINEERS', AND LIBRARIANS' CHARACTERISTICS

The following figures give the librarians' ratings of themselves, scientists, and engineers on ten of the 16PF traits and four learning preferences. The charts do no show instances in which librarians chose "no basis for opinion" or left the question blank.

Warmth

Below average Warmth was defined as "more reserved, quiet and unaffable than the average person."

Above average Warmth was defined as "more caring, friendly, and responsive to others than the average person."

Respondents could also select "about average on Warmth" or "no basis for opinion."

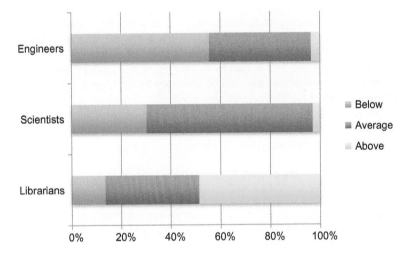

Overall, the librarians viewed themselves as Warmer than scientists or engineers, with engineers being viewed as the least Warm.

Emotional Stability

Below average Emotional Stability was defined as "more stress-prone and emotional than the average person."

Above average Emotional Stability was defined as "more quick to recover, calm and able to deal with frustrations than the average person."

Respondents could also select "about average on Emotional Stability" or "no basis for opinion."

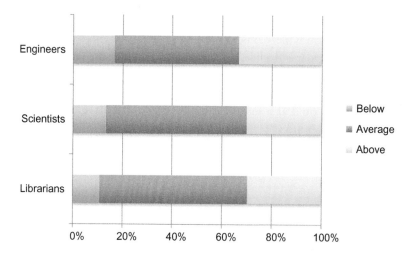

The librarians viewed themselves as slightly more Emotionally Stable than scientists or engineers, seeing none of the groups as particularly low in Emotional Stability.

Liveliness

Below average Liveliness was defined as "more sober, reflective and cautious than the average person."

Above average Liveliness was defined as "more exuberant, animated, and impulsive than the average person."

Respondents could also select "about average on Liveliness" or "no basis for opinion."

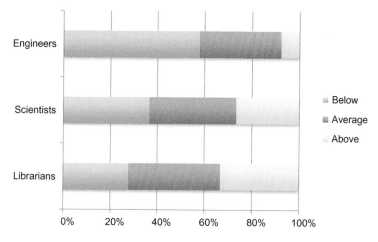

The librarians viewed themselves as more Lively than scientists or engineers, viewing engineers as the least Lively group.

Rule-Consciousness

Below average on Rule-Consciousness was defined as, "more nonconforming to group standards, flexible, and unconscientious than the average person."

Above average on Rule-Consciousness was defined as "more conforming to group standards, dependable, and responsible than the average person."

Respondents could also select "about average on Rule-Consciousness" and "no basis for opinion."

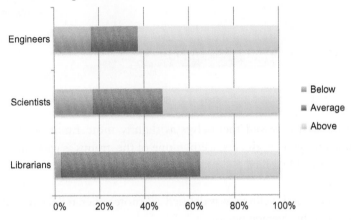

The librarians saw themselves as rather Rule-Conscious, but scientists and engineers as slightly less rule-conscious.

Sensitivity

Below average Sensitivity was defined as more "unsentimental, pragmatic, and matter-of-fact than the average person."

Above average Sensitivity was defined as "more aesthetic, empathetic, and tender-minded than the average person."

The respondents could also select "about average on Sensitivity" or "no basis for opinion."

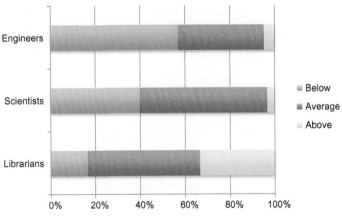

The librarians viewed themselves as more Sensitive than either scientists or engineers.

Abstractedness

Below average Abstractedness was defined as "more down to earth, practical, and literal than the average person."

Above average Abstractedness was defined as "more imaginative, fanciful, and self-absorbed than the average person."

Respondents could also choose "about average on Abstractedness" or "no basis for opinion."

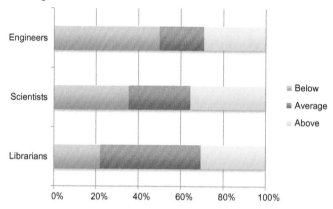

The librarians viewed engineers as somewhat less Abstracted than themselves or scientists.

Openness to Change

Below average Openness to Change was defined as "more traditional and change-resistant than the average person."

Above average Openness to Change was defined as "more open to change and open-minded than the average person."

The respondents could also select "about average on Openness to Change" or "no basis for opinion."

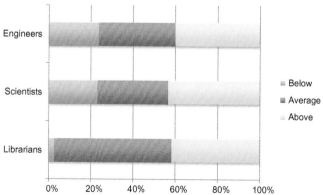

The librarians viewed themselves as somewhat more Open to Change than scientists or engineers.

Self-Reliance

Below average on Self-Reliance was defined as "more of a team player and a cooperator than the average person."

Above average on Self-Reliance was defined as "more self-sufficient and fond of autonomy than the average person."

The respondents could also select "about average on Self-Reliance" or "no basis for opinion."

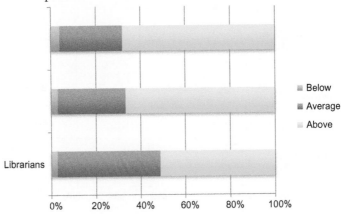

Almost all the librarians viewed all three groups as being average or above average on Self-Reliance.

Perfectionism

Below average on Perfectionism was defined as "more flexible and tolerant of disorder than the average person."

Above average on Perfectionism was defined as "more perfectionistic and organized than the average person."

The respondents could also select "about average on Perfectionism" or "no basis for opinion."

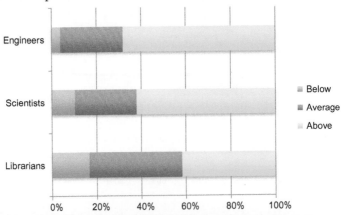

The librarians viewed themselves as somewhat less Perfectionistic than scientists or engineers.

Reasoning

Below average on Reasoning was defined as "have lower abstract problem solving person than the average person."

Above average on Reasoning was defined as "have higher abstract problem solving ability and are better at solving numerical and verbal problems than the average person."

The respondents could also select "about average on Reasoning" or "no basis for opinion."

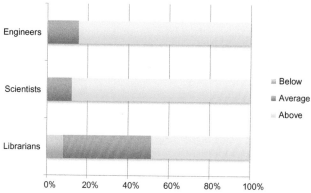

The librarians viewed scientists and engineers as being higher on the trait of Reasoning than themselves.

The librarians also indicated their perceptions of their own, scientists,' and engineers' learning preferences.

Feeling

The learning preference Feeling was defined as "learning from specific experiences and relating to people. Sensitive to others' feelings." This learning preference corresponded to Concrete Experience in Kolb's framework. Librarians could choose "no basis for opinion," as well.

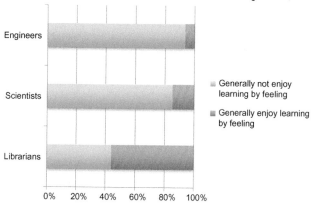

The librarians considered themselves to be higher on Feeling than either scientists or engineers.

Watching

Watching was defined as "observing before making a judgment by viewing the environment from different perspectives. Looks for the meaning of things." Watching corresponded to Reflective Observation in Kolb's framework. The librarians could choose "no basis for opinion."

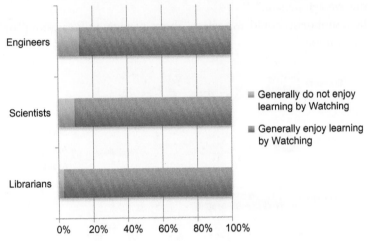

Librarians viewed all three groups as predominantly enjoying learning by Watching.

Thinking

Thinking was defined as "logical analysis of ideas and acting on Intellectual understanding of a situation." This corresponded to Abstract Conceptualization in Kolb's framework. "No basis for opinion" was also a choice.

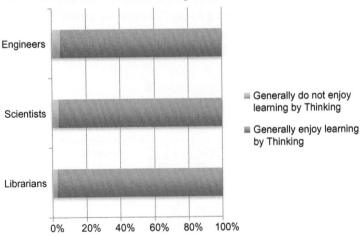

All three groups were seen as enjoying Thinking by the librarians.
Doing

Doing was defined as "ability to get things done by influencing people and events through actions. Includes risk-taking." This corresponded to Active Experimentation in Kolb's framework. "No basis for opinion" was another choice.

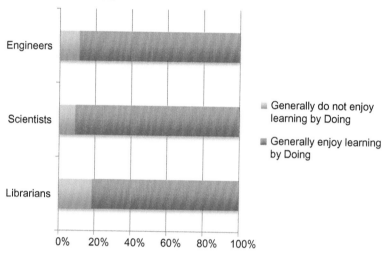

Most librarians viewed all three groups as enjoying learning by Doing.

7.3 CONCLUSION

As this chapter has shown, librarians have a variety of attitudes towards the personalization of instruction and communication to personality traits and learning preferences of scientists and engineers. In addition, librarians at times rate themselves differently than scientists and engineers in respect to the ten 16PF personality traits that I included in the survey. While a possible methodological caveat is that the ratings were only based on a few descriptors, rather than the entire 16PF test, it is at least interesting to note librarians' rough opinions of themselves and their clientele. The next chapter discusses several practical applications of personality traits and learning styles to library instruction in the sciences and engineering.

REFERENCE

Coffield, F., Moseley, D., Hall, E., & Ecclestone, K. (2004). *Learning styles and pedagogy in post 16 learning: A systematic and critical review.* London: The Learning and Skills Research Centre.

CHAPTER 8

Applications

8.1 USING THE KOLB LEARNING CYCLE

Because the cognitive activity involved in learning is not directly observable, I cannot conclude with certainty that Kolb's model is an accurate model of what goes on inside an individual's brain when he or she learns, but the model does have face validity in that it includes ways in which people engage with learning. For example, I am aware that both reflection and action (learning by doing) are approaches to learning that can be beneficial. Similarly, I can see that a Concrete Experience often may prompt me to engage in learning and lead to my looking for generalizable (abstract) information related to that experience.

I and the other instructors who have used the Kolb model to plan instruction believe that it can lead to a rich, well-rounded learning experience that encourages students to approach learning problem from several angles: they experience the problem for themselves or reflect on similar experiences in their lives; they learn about abstract knowledge related to the problem; they practice solving the problem based on this knowledge; and eventually they are able to solve similar problems independently in the real world. The Kolb model has the benefit of including both learning by doing and reflection, both of which have been seen as beneficial in the engineering pedagogical literature (Cowan, 2006; Prince, 2004).

A method that has been used to apply the Kolb learning styles model has been to provide activities corresponding to four stages of a "learning cycle," which in Kolb's view represented the complete learning process. There have been criticisms of the learning cycle approach:

Kolb clearly believes that learning takes place in a cycle and that learners should use all four phases of that cycle to become effective. Popular adaptations of his theory (for which he is not, of course, responsible) claim, however, that all four phases should be tackled and in order. The manual for the third version of the LSI is explicit on this point: 'You may begin a learning process in any of the four phases of the learning cycle. Ideally, using a well-rounded learning process, you would cycle through all the four phases. However, you may find that you sometimes skip a phase in the cycle or focus primarily on just one' (Kolb, 1999, p. 4). But if Wierstra

Teaching to Individual Differences in Science and Engineering Librarianship
http://dx.doi.org/10.1016/B978-0-08-101881-1.00008-X

and de Jong's (2002) analysis, which reduces Kolb's model to a one-dimensional bipolar structure of reflection versus doing, proves to be accurate, then the notion of a learning cycle may be seriously flawed (Coffield, Moseley, Hall, & Ecclestone, 2004).

I present an example of a lesson plan that tackles the four stages in order, so that I can illustrate activities that can be used with the various learning styles. However, I do not advocate for always teaching to the stages in this order, and I am open to the fact that it may be important primarily to include a balance of reflective and active components in instruction. It may also be important to include a "connective component" that engages students in the material, since connective instruction has been shown to predict student engagement more than seven times as much as academically rigorous or lively teaching (Cooper, 2014). "Connective instruction," according to Cooper, "is a category of teaching practices in which teachers help students to make personal connections to a class." (2014, p. 366). I discuss a connective activity in the first stage of the learning cycle-based lesson plan below.

The method used for constructing this lesson plan is 4MAT (McCarthy & McCarthy, 2006). Although Coffield et al. (2004) criticized the 4MAT system for lack of evidence for some of its claims, I use it here because following its' methods results in including activities for Kolb's four learning styles types. It also provides "stretch" activities for all learning styles and a variety in instructional techniques that I personally found lacking in my own instruction before using the system. While I agree with the engineering educator Cowan (2006) that learning does not always proceed in the four-quadrant order described in some learning cycle approaches (there may be looping back between different stages), the four stage approach does allow someone new to the Kolb model to see easily what activities may be associated with different learning style preferences. In addition, systems like 4MAT derived from the Kolb framework can offer practical ways to apply Kolb's theory.

In addition, the Kolb model and the 4MAT system place a strong emphasis on the connective element in instruction, which is directly addressed in Quadrant 1 of 4MAT, or the quadrant including Concrete Experience and Reflective Observation in Kolb's model. While connecting with the student should not be confined to Quadrant 1 alone, but should happen throughout the instruction, what is notable about the Kolb model and 4MAT is that they recognize the importance of this element of instruction.

8.1.1 A Learning Cycle Based Lesson Plan

Let us turn to a specific example of a lesson plan that I created using the 4MAT system. This example was inspired by Fosmire and Radcliffe's book,

Integrating Information into the Engineering Design Process, which addresses teaching students in engineering design classes how to get and incorporate information needed at different stages of the design process (2014).

8.1.1.1 Design Framework

The class content is "Information Needed at Different Stages of the Design Process." The "Essential Question"[17] is "What information is needed at the different stages of the design process?"

Desired outcomes are that students will know stages of the design cycle and information types associated with these; that they will plan ways to find information at one of these stages; and that they will be aware of the importance of information throughout all stages of the design process.

8.1.1.2 Instructional Delivery

This section of the lesson plan includes the instructional activities I included for 4MAT's eight instructional stages (two for each Kolb quadrant). While it may not be necessary to teach all eight stages in some classes, I incorporated them all here for purpose of illustration.

1. Connect: Connecting to the Concept Experientially (Quadrant 1-Round Thinking)
   Each student shares with a fellow student a time in his or her life when lacking information resulted in a suboptimal outcome, and how this felt.
2. Attend: Attending to the Connection (Quadrant 1-Linear Thinking)
   In pairs, students discuss commonalities and differences of how having the information would have helped.
3. Image: Creating a Mental Picture (Quadrant 2-Round Thinking)
   Students are presented with the following statement and asked to fill it in. "The result of missing information is_____."
4. Inform: Receiving Facts and Knowledge (Quadrant 2-Linear Thinking)
   The librarian gives a lecture on stages of the design cycle and how to find information needed during these stages.

---

[17] The 4MAT system recommends having an "essential question" to guide a class that all parts of the class should be related to. Note that the 4MAT model also breaks each of Kolb's quadrants into two parts exemplifying "round" and "linear" thinking. Connect, Image, Extend, and Perform are all "round" activities involving more creative, nonlinear thinking. Attend, Inform, Practice, and Refine are "linear" activities. While I do not know whether it is always beneficial to incorporate activities for both kinds of thinking in each of Kolb's quadrants, doing so does result in great variety in instructional techniques, and the founder of 4MAT, Bernice McCarthy, considers it important to do so (personal communication).

5. Practice: Developing Skills (Quadrant 3-Linear Thinking)
   Students do a matching exercise of examples of information and stages of the design process.
6. Extend: Extending Learning to the Outside World (Quadrant 3-Round Thinking)
   Students pick a stage of the design process and plan how to find information needed for that stage.
7. Refine: Refining the Extension (Quadrant 4-Linear Thinking)
   Students share their plans on a whiteboard and the class discusses them.
8. Perform: Creative Manifestation of Material Learned (Quadrant 4-Round Thinking)
   After the class, students find information for their current design problem and give feedback to the librarian about what the design team still needs to know.

To address time considerations, the librarian may want to ask students to read materials outside or class, or he or she may want to give handouts to students during the lecture. In my view it is important not to cram so much information into the lecture that the class neglects the elements of connecting with the student or getting students to think about applying the information in real world situations. My past classes tended to be very lecture-heavy and learning about the Kolb framework has convinced me of the importance of other learning processes than just receiving information.

8.2 PLANNING INSTRUCTION THAT ADAPTS TO PERSONALITY CHARACTERISTICS

Five personality traits will be discussed in this section: Introversion, emotional stability, Openness, intrinsic motivation, and reasoning.

As Chapter 4 showed, librarians, scientists, and engineers, as groups, tend to be introverted, although there will be exceptions to the rule. Thus it is important to examine how Introversion can affect teaching and learning, and how to adapt instruction to this trait if necessary. A book by Denis Lawrence discussed how teachers who were introverted, and/or who had high emotionality, could teach with confidence and increase their self-esteem (1999). Lawrence stated that teaching was predominantly an Extraverted profession, but that Introverted teachers could adapt, for example, by incorporating one-on-one teaching in their instruction. Other writers, such as Cain, do not consider Introversion to be a detriment to teaching, although Introverts may need to recharge from the extensive social interaction in this profession (2013).

Introverted students may not enjoy some cooperative group work activities. Novicki (2016); however, states that there are some kinds of group work that everyone can enjoy. Characteristics of group work in which "all can thrive" include:

- "structured activities that build in equal participation and prevent Dominance
- students work in small groups instead of entire class discussions
- time is allotted for students to think individually before responding
- reminders to students to take turns, listen without interrupting, and paraphrase what others say
- activities are timed, and students reminded to switch speakers
- students assigned clear roles for the activities"

Librarians who want to ensure participation from all their students may want to consider using Think-Pair-Shares, since these would probably not be uncomfortable for most introverted students (Cain, 2013). Entire class discussions, on the other hand, have not been successful in the engineering classes that I have taught. Other activities that would appeal to introverted students are "Quick-Write" activities such as journaling or minute papers.

Emotional stability is another personality trait that significantly affects teaching and learning. A study of teachers in Hong Kong and Shanghai found that teaching anxiety was predicted by trait anxiety, which is anxiety that is not related just to a particular situation, but that is characteristic of an individual (Cheung & Hui, 2011). Anxiety is negatively correlated with the Big Five personality trait of Emotional Stability (Kotov, Gamez, Schmidt, & Watson, 2010). Trait anxiety in Cheung and Hui's study was associated with the teaching anxiety factors of incompetence in the classroom, incompetence to speak up, fear of observation, dislike of teaching, and career uncertainty, as well as negative self-esteem. Cheung and Hui cite Keavney and Sinclair (1978), who found that teaching anxiety negatively impacted survival in the teaching profession, affective impact in the classroom, student achievement, and the teacher's coping skills. The classroom atmosphere may be less warm when teachers have high teaching anxiety, and students themselves may become more anxious, resulting in hostility between the students and the teacher. In addition, Keavney and Sinclair found that academic achievement was lower when teachers had high teaching anxiety, and that teachers sometimes adopted a dogmatic teaching style to cope with their anxiety.

Librarians who score low on Emotional Stability and high on Apprehension would be expected to create a less warm classroom atmosphere, and perhaps to make students more anxious. Since librarians often meet students in just one class session, it is important for them to make the impression that they are approachable and willing to help. Using public speaking anxiety reduction tips may help (Anderson, 2016).

Students with low Emotional Stability also have challenges in learning situations. Deziel, Olawo, Truchon, and Golab (2013) at the University of Waterloo found that engineering students' mental health, as defined by ability to enjoy life, resilience, balance, emotional flexibility, and self-actualization, was affected by factors such as a student's year of study, hours of homework, major, and gender. First year and final year students had the lowest mental health, and females had lower overall mental health than male students. Students in more competitive programs such as electrical engineering had lower mental health than those in programs like Systems Design where there were strong relationships among classmates and a more flexible curriculum. Thus engineering students face a number of possible stressors, such as their heavy workload, sometimes competitive relationships, and differential experiences due to gender. Students with lower emotional stability would be expected to fare less well in terms of mental health since they have lower resilience.

Librarians can mitigate student anxiety by creating a warm classroom climate and teaching about resources to make their research work flows more efficient, such as bibliographic management software. In addition, librarians need to be sensitive to the time pressure faced by engineering students and work toward removing barriers that students sometimes face when using library resources to complete their assignments.

Openness to Change and/or Openness to Experience are positive traits for teaching and learning that librarians, scientists, and engineers typically score high in, compared to the norm populations. High Openness to Change and Openness to Experience are associated with liking to think about things in new ways and being creative. Individuals who score high on these traits often like learning new things. In addition, teachers with high scores on Openness tend to be engaged with their subject matter and curious.

I believe that high Openness can compensate for learning challenges that may be presented by low Extraversion and low Emotional Stability. A teacher who is passionate about his or her subject matter can convey enthusiasm even if he or she is not naturally high in Liveliness. Similarly, engineering and science students high in Openness may be particularly receptive to learning about tools that can equip them for lifelong learning, such as current awareness RSS feeds, patents databases, and searchable ebook collections. Sources that allow science and engineering students to satisfy their curiosity and expand their knowledge would be expected to be appealing to them due to their high Openness.

Engineers and scientists typically have high degrees of intrinsic work motivation, meaning that they value intrinsic aspects of the work itself more than extrinsic rewards (Lounsbury et al., 2012; Williamson, Lounsbury, & Han, 2013). Similarly to Openness, Intrinsic Motivation can mitigate low Extraversion and low Emotional Stability, in my opinion. Engineers and scientists who enjoy their subject matter would be expected to be receptive to learning about tools that would be useful in engineering or scientific problem solving. Students' high Intrinsic Motivation would most likely contribute to engagement that librarians could leverage by connecting library instruction to the problems that engineering and science students are learning to solve.

Strictly speaking, Reasoning is not a personality trait, but since it is one of the factors measured by the 16PF, I discuss it here. Need for Cognition, that is, enjoyment of thinking and mental activity (Hill et al., 2013), is moderately associated with intelligence (which is measured by Reasoning). Need for Cognition is also associated with high Openness to Experience and Conscientiousness (Sadowski & Cogburn, 1997). Park, Baker, and Lee (2008) showed that Korean civil engineers' Need for Cognition interacted with task complexity in predicting job satisfaction. Thus the engineers required challenging tasks to be satisfied with their jobs. Similarly, library instruction for science and engineering students needs to be challenging to match these students' high levels of Reasoning and Openness. Interactive exercises that make students think, for example, Quick-Write activities such as minute papers; discussions in Think-Share-Pairs; and introductions to challenging search tools such as SciFinder or SureChemBL, would beneficially supplement simple lectures on "library logistics." Even if science and engineering students lack rudimentary logistical knowledge about the library, perhaps this can be communicated with handouts so that precious class time can be used to stimulate higher order mental processes.

8.3 CONSIDERATIONS FOR DIFFERENT KINDS OF ENGINEERING AND SCIENCE CLASSES

8.3.1 Undergraduate

Smith, Sekar, and Townsend (2002) described a curriculum recommending that beginning/general level science students learn about basic information literacy skills, basic types of information in the sciences, selected core resources for a scientific subject area, the basic research process, basic search skills, applying search skills, evaluating print and web resources, citing works, and citation formats in the sciences. Thus at the beginning level library instruction would focus on factual information and development of basic skills.

In the Kolb model, factual information is communicated at the Abstract Conceptualization-Reflective Observation quadrant of the learning cycle, and skills building belongs to the Abstract Conceptualization-Active Experimentation quadrant. While both of these stages would be familiar to engineering and science students who tend to be Assimilators and Convergers, I wonder if focusing primarily on factual knowledge and basic skills leaves out the important basic step of forming a connection between students' experiences and the library research process. Students who are not convinced of the value of library resources and librarians for their development as scientists and engineers may continue to use the easiest way out of finding information (Google). It may be a beneficial "stretch" for students' learning to engage in Concrete Experience-Reflective Observation activities linking the library instruction subject matter to their experiences (the first quadrant of Kolb's cycle).

From a practical standpoint, in my experience beginning/general engineering classes have been large, so both reflective and active exercises have to be adapted to this factor. For the reflective component of the class, I have found minute papers (Vella, 2015) to be especially effective. For example, during a large introductory lecture to Mechanical, Aerospace, and Biomedical Engineering students, I asked students to reflect on and write about a time when they found too much information and a time when they found too little information. I then gave a lecture on strategies to improve searches in order to narrow and broaden their results. The "active" portion of the class involved having the students suggest topics and how they would search for information on these topics (during a class discussion). If I were going to do it over, I would have had students form into Think-Pair-Shares for this segment of the class, which might have been more effective than a general class discussion. Although it would have been impractical to have students work individually or in pairs on laptops, I think the Think-Pair-Shares where students strategized about searching would have been a feasible substitute. A few of the Think-Pair-Share search process strategies could have been shared with the larger class and brief feedback could be provided. The Accommodation quadrant of Kolb's learning cycle (Concrete Experience-Active Experimentation) was met by asking students to apply their new search skills in the real-world application of gathering sources for a technical paper. This part was conducted out of class.

Personality traits, as well as learning styles, can also be taken into broad consideration in large introductory classes like the MABE one in this example. The reflective minute papers are helpful for students low on Extraversion as would be Think-Share-Pairs. Being careful not to be critical of individual students' contributions would be helpful in modeling a "safe" classroom environment for any students low in emotional stability. Exposure to new search strategies might appeal to students high in Openness to Experience or Openness to Change. Connecting the library instruction subject matter to students' own academic experiences would probably have helped students high on intrinsic motivation.

8.3.2 Graduate Classes

Graduate classes in the sciences and engineering typically orient students to library services and introduce the librarian to them. Another approach is to offer classes on literature reviews, bibliographic management, or other topics. Graduate classes often have many more international students than undergraduate classes. While the same basic personality traits, such as the Big Five personality traits of Openness, Conscientiousness, Extraversion, Agreeableness, and Neuroticism are believed to be universal (McCrae & Costa, 1997), it is not clear whether international science and engineering students have the same personality and learning styles profile as their US counterparts. Overall, people in East Asian countries—to give one example—are less Extraverted, Agreeable, Conscientious, and Open to Experience than people in other world regions, and higher in Neuroticism (Schmitt, Allik, McCrae, & Benet-Martinez, 2007). However, one cannot generalize about individuals from country statistics. Librarians should be aware that international students may as a whole differ from US undergraduate students in regards to their personality characteristics.

In addition, possibly due to cultural factors, some international students may be unwilling to ask for help from a librarian. Language difficulties may also discourage some international students from asking questions.

Because of these factors, it is important for librarians to establish a connection with international graduate students at the outset. Written materials may be helpful for students with language difficulties, as well as web pages. As with undergraduates, a connection can be established by making graduate students aware of tools that can make their life easier, which for graduate students might include bibliographic management applications, plagiarism detection software, full text resources, and interlibrary loan.

Participation exercises such as Think-Pair-Shares that work with undergraduates may not go over as well with graduate students, particularly international ones who may be more accustomed to a lecture format. Perhaps the most important thing is to engage in a dialog with graduate students to find out about their needs. To make those graduate students who are Introverted more comfortable, the librarian could ask students to write down their questions and then the librarian could address these in his or her lecture.

8.3.3 Engineering Design Classes

This section will discuss how engineering and science students' personality characteristics and learning styles may affect learning how to obtain various kinds of information needed in the design process. Two chapters in Radcliffe and Fosmire's book, *Integrating Information into the Engineering Design Process* (2014), are sources for this section.

First, in her chapter "Find the Real Need," Nelson provides suggestions for engineering design students to use in ascertaining requirements from clients, users, and other stakeholders such as conducting interviews and doing observations (2014). Nelson makes the point that engineering students often do not learn such communication skills in their curriculum.

The active listening and observation of body language that are helpful for interviews with stakeholders may not come naturally to those engineering students who are low on Extraversion and Sensitivity. Drawing out others in conversation is probably easier for outgoing individuals. Also, individuals with higher levels of Sensitivity tend to be more empathetic than more grounded people, and being empathetic would assist in understanding others during interviews.

Nelson's chapter gives students some good suggestions for how to develop communication skills that I argue may not come naturally to some engineers. Another approach on a design team would be to assign the facilitation of interviews to those engineering students who have more natural ability with active listening.

Garritano, in his chapter "Making Dependable Decisions," recommends to students that they learn to use structured analysis methods to determine the relevance and reputability of sources of information (2014). For example, he recommends doing a pro/con evaluation of a source's benefits and drawbacks and he also gives a useful list of criteria that can be used to evaluate sources. Structured analysis methods like these should be appealing to engineers who probably encounter similar kinds of tools in their engineering curriculum. In addition, these kinds of methods probably appeal to engineering students who are high on the trait of Tough-Mindedness, which is associated with enjoying logical analysis. These methods may also appeal to engineering students who have converging or assimilating learning styles since the analysis involves Abstract Conceptualization.

8.3.4 Online Instruction

STEM librarians increasingly are embedded in courses, many of which are online, or may teach their own for credit online information literacy courses (Pritchard, 2010; York & Vance, 2009). Online instruction, which is increasingly prevalent in higher education with the rise of distance education classes, offers different instructional experiences for students than in-person instruction. Preference for these experiences is in part a product of personality characteristics and learning style.

The National Center for Education Statistics in the US reported that 27.1% of the students in postsecondary institutions were taking at least one distance education class in Fall 2013 (2016). About 16% of undergraduates were taking distance education course in 2003–04, and around 21% in 2007–08. Fully 32% of undergraduates were taking an online course in 2011–12. There was a drop in the percentage of undergraduates taking distance education courses in Fall, 2013 (to about 27%), but about 31% of postbaccalaureate students were taking distance education courses at that time.

U.S. News and World Report found that about 28% of the institutions it surveyed during a collection period in 2015 had online Master's programs in engineering fields (Brooks & Morse, 2016). *Learning at a Distance*, a report of the US Department of Education, found that in 2008 undergraduates in natural sciences and engineering enrolled in online degree programs less frequently than the average for undergraduates in all fields of study, however (Radford, 2011). Undergraduates in computer and information sciences were enrolled in online degree programs more often than the average for other fields of study.

Given these statistics, one would expect many graduate students in engineering and the sciences to take distance learning courses, and increasingly, undergraduates in certain courses. Reaching these distance learning students would require either participating in online course sessions; meeting with individuals using Zoom or similar software; embedding information in course management systems like Blackboard; or producing web pages. Personality characteristics and learning styles affect Internet use and impressions of preferences of online courses as well as participation in asynchronous and synchronous discussions.

8.3.5 Personality Characteristics Involved in Online Instruction

8.3.5.1 Internet Use

A recent study of more than 6900 young adults (Mark & Ganzach, 2014) found that Extraversion, Neuroticism, and Conscientiousness were positively correlated with Internet use. Some of the findings in this study contradict earlier studies with smaller samples. Mark and Ganzach explain that extraverts may enjoy using the Internet because of the range of externally stimulating features it provides. Neurotic individuals may use the Internet to search for information to allay anxiety, or to get online help for depression. Highly Conscientious people may use the Internet for forming plans or organizing.

8.3.5.2 Preference for Online Courses or Other Academic Internet Use

Mark and Ganzach (2014) found a positive correlation between Extraversion, Openness, and Neuroticism and online academic activities. They explained that Extraverts may tend to seek stimulation through learning; Open individuals may expand their interests by taking online courses; and Neurotic people may find online courses less anxiety-provoking due to being able to work privately at their own pace.

Keller and Karau (2013) studied the relationship between personality characteristics and online course impressions and found that Conscientiousness and work experience were positive predictors of their overall evaluation of online courses. Conscientiousness and academic level were predictors of preference for online courses, with more Conscientious people preferring online courses and with undergraduates preferring online courses more than graduate students. Engagement with online courses was positively predicted by work experience and Conscientiousness. Perceptions of online courses' value to one's career were positively predicted by work experience, Conscientiousness, Agreeableness, and Openness. Anxiety/frustration with online courses was negatively predicted by work experience, marital status (with married people being less anxious/frustrated with online courses), and Conscientiousness. Notably, Keller and Karau's study pertained just to impressions of online courses, whereas Mark and Ganzach' study measured online academic activities in general (both research and online course participation). Landers and Lounsbury (2006) found that in a sample of 117 undergraduates, Conscientiousness was positively correlated with percent of Internet usage for academic purposes. Thus more Conscientious undergraduates devoted a greater proportion of their overall Internet usage to academic purposes. Mark and Ganzach's study included all types of young adults, not just college students, in contrast to the studies by Keller and Karau and Landers and Lounsbury.

Overall, based on these conclusions, the librarian might expect that students in online courses could be more Extraverted, Open, and Neurotic than the general population of young adults, but that more Conscientious students might have more positive impressions of online courses. However, librarians should keep in mind that the students in online engineering and science courses are coming from the population of science and engineering students, not just young adults or college students in general. Thus they may be similar to other science and engineering students in terms of personality.

8.3.5.3 Email and Online Class Behaviors

Hertel, Schroer, Batinic, and Naumann found that more Introverted and Neurotic individuals preferred email over face-to-face communication (2008). Extraverts preferred face-to-face communication more than email.

Pavalache-Ilie and Cocorada found that in a sample of engineering students, Introverts in online classes did not enjoy online group work as much as Extraverts did, and that they needed more guidance from the teacher when doing group work (2014). Ghorbani and Montazer found that Extraverts participated more often in chat rooms and forums and made more posts in forums in an online class (2015). They also had more friends in an online learning environment.

The other Big Five personality traits were involved in behavior in online learning environments as well. Ghorbani and Montazer (2015) found that Neurotic students had fewer friends, entered the system less often per week, and had less delay in delivering assignments. Students high in Openness had more friends, greater difficulty level of examples and exercises, more time dedicated to reading concepts and theories, and more time dedicated to reading about examples and cases. More Agreeable students participated more often in chat rooms and forums and in troubleshooting groups. More Conscientious students had a lower delay in delivering assignments, entered the system more frequently during a week, had higher scores, and viewed the lesson news more often.

An implication of these studies' findings is that personality can be expected to affect a number of online class behaviors. Librarians who are embedded in online courses or teaching their own for-credit online courses should especially be aware that Introverted and Neurotic students may need greater support, since they tend to participate less often in online course discussions and have fewer class friends. It may be that Introverted and Neurotic individuals will be comfortable emailing librarians, however.

8.3.5.4 Getting Clues About Personality in Emails and Online Posts

Emails and online posts do not have the richness of face-to-face communication, but studies of linguistic markers of personality can inform librarians' understanding of textual communications from students. While the correlations between linguistic markers and personality traits such as the Big Five traits, Conscientiousness, Openness, Neuroticism, Agreeableness, and Extraversion, are small, they are statistically significant (Mairesse, Walker, Mehl, & Moore, 2007; Pennebaker & King, 1999). While a librarian cannot form definite conclusions about students' personality traits from their emails and entries in threaded discussions, he or she can at least form working hypotheses about the students' personality characteristics.

Pennebaker and King (1999) found that there were significant correlations between the Big Five personality traits and linguistic features measured by the Linguistic Inquiry and Word Count software program (LIWC). LIWC, originally developed by Pennebaker and his colleagues (Pennebaker, 2011; Pennebaker, Booth, & Francis, 2001), measures the percentage in a text of a number of linguistic features, such as pronouns and causation words (e.g., "because," "reason," and "why"), to name just two categories. In their exploratory analysis, Pennebaker and King (1999) ran the LIWC on more than a thousand introductory psychology students' reflective essays. Correlations between the students' scores on a Five Factor personality test and the LIWC frequencies for selected linguistic feature were calculated.

Neuroticism was positively correlated with the percentage of first-person singular pronouns and negative emotion words, but negatively correlated with the percentage of articles (like "a" and "the") and positive emotion words. Extraversion was positively correlated with positive emotion words and social words, but negatively correlated with articles, exclusive words (such as "but," "without," and "except"), tentativity words, and negation words. Openness was positively correlated with articles, words of more than six letters, exclusive words, tentativity words, and insight words (such as "know" and "realize"); but negatively correlated with first-person singular words, present tense, and causation words. Agreeableness was positively correlated with first person singular and positive emotion words, but negatively correlated with words of more than six letters and negative emotion words.

Conscientiousness was positively correlated with positive emotion words and negatively correlated with discrepancies (such as "should," "would," and "could"), exclusive words, negations, causation words, and negative emotion words.

8.3.5.5 In-person Discussions

Mairesse et al. (2007) summarized research on differences between introverts' and extraverts' oral language cues. Verbal features of Introverts that Mairesse summarized include: self-focused topic selection, problem talk (dissatisfaction), strict selection of topics, single topic selection, few semantic errors, and few self-references. In addition, the style used by Introverts is formal and has many tentativity words. There are also many nouns, adjectives, prepositions, elaborated constructions, words per sentence, articles, and negations. The lexicon of Introverts is correct, rich, has high diversity, and has many exclusive and inclusive words and many negative emotion words. Their lexicon also has few social words and positive emotion words.

Extraverts, on the other hand, produce more pleasure talk, agreement, and compliments. They also select many topics, make many semantic errors, and have many self-references. They use many verbs, adverbs, and implicit pronouns. They use few words per sentence, few articles, and few negations. They have a poor lexicon with low diversity, few exclusive and inclusive words, and few negative emotion words. They use many social and positive emotion words.

Nonverbal language cues shown by introverts included more listening and less back-channel behavior (such as using expressions such as hmm or uh huh). Introverts also spoke more quietly with more unfilled pauses and lower vocal frequency variability.[18] Extraverts initiated conversation more often and exhibited more back-channel behavior. They had a higher speech rate with fewer unfilled pauses. They were also louder and had higher vocal frequency variability.

These findings suggest that it may be reasonable to form hypotheses about whether students are Introverted or Extraverted in synchronous online or in-person discussions. Textual asynchronous communications can stimulate the librarian to form hypotheses about students' personality traits, as well. For example, if the student's post included many words over six letters, I might suspect that he or she had a high level of Openness. If a

---

[18]Mairesse et al. also found other nonverbal differences between introverts and extraverts, but the reader is encouraged to consult the original article for these.

student used first person singular pronouns frequently, I might wonder if he or she was high on Neuroticism. Since less Emotionally Stable students tend to need more support in online learning situations, there is practical significance in trying to identify these students from their communications.

8.3.5.6 How the Librarian Can Support Students in Online Environments

When the librarian is embedded in online classes, he or she can have a positive effect on students, regardless of their personality characteristics. By maintaining a public presence on a course site, the librarian can encourage Introverted students to reach out for help, and allay some of the anxiety that Neurotic students may be facing. Two techniques can be useful to the librarian for maintaining a helpful presence in online courses: projecting a sense of his or her own personality, and engaging to some extent in language style matching with students in written communications, in order to establish rapport with them.

Chepya (2005) advocates showing "e-personality" in an online course. According to Chepya it is possible to create a human, companionable element online, just as one can do this in a traditional classroom. Teacher immediacy—the degree of psychological distance the teacher puts between himself or herself and his or her object of communication—is an important component of students' satisfaction with online courses and may contribute to learning as well (Richardson & Swan, 2003). The librarian needs to engage in interactions with students in online courses to show social presence. Baker (2010) has some additional tips for showing immediacy:

> Established verbally immediate behaviors include initiating discussions, asking questions, using self-disclosure, addressing students by name, using inclusive personal pronouns (we, us), repeating contacts with students over time, responding frequently to students, offering praise, and communicating attentiveness (O'Sullivan, Hunt, & Lippert, 2004). The researchers also noted that visual cues (e.g., color, graphics, or an instructor's picture) signal expressiveness, accessibility, engagement, and politeness. The online learning environment allows instructors to incorporate verbally immediate behaviors easily with careful design of the course content and written interactions with students.

The librarian needs to give a sense of himself or herself as expressive, accessible, engaged, and polite. Providing biographical material in his or her profile and interacting frequently with students online can help the librarian to achieve this.

The librarian may also want to engage in a degree of language style matching with students in written communications, as well, although I would caution that this has to be done in a natural way. Language style matching is similarity between individuals' discourse in linguistic features. One way language style matching has been measured has been using the LIWC, mentioned above, which counts the frequencies of more than 70 linguistic categories.

Ireland et al. (2011) showed that language style matching, as measured by function words such as pronouns and articles, was a strong predictor of relationship initiation in a speed dating experiment. It also predicted relationship stability (couples' satisfaction with the relationship and tendency to stay in the relationship). While clearly librarians are in a different setting than that studied by Ireland et al., the idea that language style matching can affect collaborators' satisfaction with each other has been borne out. Gonzales et al. (2009) found that language style matching in both face-to-face groups and online groups predicted group cohesion in groups engaged in an information search task. Language style matching also increased task performance in the face-to-face group engaging in the information search task.

Language style matching is usually an unconscious process. Manson, Bryant, Gervais, and Kline (2013) say that it is a form of behavioral coordination. Citing several studies, Manson et al. state:

> Coordinated language use and behavior may facilitate mutual understanding (Pickering & Garrod, 2004). Ireland and Pennebaker (2010; see also Meyer & Bock, 1999) argued that function words such as pronouns and articles (unlike content words) are "inherently social," because their comprehension typically depends, not just on the conventions of a speech community, but also on shared frames of reference actively established among interlocutors.

How, then, can the librarian use language style matching without doing so in an obviously artificial way? I would argue that the librarian could easily use the same pronouns that students use in their written communication. If the student says:

> I need some information on the Golden Gate Bridge.

The librarian could respond:

> I will be happy to help you. I am pretty sure there is some information in Compendex. I will check and get back to you.

Instead of

> Compendex most likely has that kind of information. Go to the library databases page...

Similarly, if the general tone of the student's message is formal, the librarian can respond formally. If the student is more casual or discloses personal information, the librarian can respond in a warm way, such as by saying, "have a good weekend."

8.3.6 Learning Styles Characteristics Involved in Online Instruction

In an early study of the relationship between Kolb learning styles and web-based instruction, Federico (2000) found that Assimilators and Accommodators had more favorable attitudes towards aspects of web-based instruction than Convergers or Divergers. Terrell (2002) found that students preferring Concrete Experience (Divergers and Accommodators) were more likely to drop out of a web-based Computing Technology in Education class. Students favoring Abstract Conceptualization were more likely to complete the class.

Fahy and Ally (2005) found differences between the ways that students with different learning styles communicated in an online class. Convergers made more postings that were also longer than the postings by Divergers. Accommodators produced more statements related to maintaining the health of the social network than the less feeling-oriented Assimilators did. These included engaging and scaffolding statement, which "initiate or sustain dialogue, and include others by encouraging, reaching out, thanking, recognizing, and acknowledging others' contributions."

Although these studies provide some evidence that learning styles affect aspects of web-based learning, Santo (2006) cites several studies that fail to show a relationship between Kolb learning styles and online course learning variables. In addition, I could not find any studies on detection of Kolb learning styles, although there were some on the Felder-Silverman Index of Learning Styles model (e.g., Graf & Kinshuk, 2006). Overall, based on this lack of evidence, it seems more appropriate to personalize e-learning to personality characteristics than Kolb learning styles.

8.4 CONCLUSION

This section has shown that personality characteristics are correlated with aspects of online course experience. It may be possible to make inferences about personality traits from posts and emails in online course sites from linguistic markers. The librarian who is embedded in an online course, or who is the instructor, should give a sense of his or her own personality with immediacy behaviors, and may want to engage in language style matching with the students' discourse, as long as this is not too artificial. In addition, this chapter has given several recommendations for personalizing in-person instruction using Kolb learning styles and personality traits. The next chapter considers the librarian's use of knowledge about his or her own personality traits to reflectively improve instruction.

REFERENCES

Anderson, C. (2016). *TED talks: The official TED guide to public speaking.* Boston, MA: Houghton Mifflin Harcourt.

Baker, C. (2010). The impact of instructor immediacy and presence for online student affective learning, cognition, and motivation. *Journal of Educators Online, 7*(1), n1. http://dx.doi.org/10.9743/JEO.2010.1.2.

Brooks, E., & Morse, R. (2016). *Methodology: Best online engineering programs rankings.* Retrieved from http://www.usnews.com/education/online-education/articles/engineering-methodology.

Cain, S. (2013). *Quiet: The power of introverts in a world that can't stop talking.* New York, NY: Broadway Books.

Chepya, P. (2005). E-personality: The fusion of it and pedagogical technique. *Educause Quarterly, 28*(3), 9.

Cheung, H.Y., & Hui, S. K. (2011). Teaching anxiety amongst Hong Kong and Shanghai in-service teachers: The impact of trait anxiety and self-esteem. *Asia-Pacific Education Researcher (De La Salle University Manila), 20*(2),395–409.

Coffield, F., Moseley, D., Hall, E., & Ecclestone, K. (2004). *Learning styles and pedagogy in post 16 learning: A systematic and critical review.* London: The Learning and Skills Research Centre.

Cooper, K. S. (2014). Eliciting engagement in the high school classroom a mixed-methods examination of teaching practices. *American Educational Research Journal, 51*(2), 363–402. http://dx.doi.org/10.3102/0002831213507973.

Cowan, J. (2006). *On becoming an innovative university teacher: Reflection in action* (2nd ed.). New York, NY: Society for Research into Higher Education & Open University Press.

Deziel, M., Olawo, D., Truchon, L., & Golab, L. (2013). *Analyzing the mental health of engineering students using classification and regression.* Paper presented at the International Educational Mining Society.

Fahy, P. J., & Ally, M. (2005). Student learning style and asynchronous computer-mediated conferencing (cmc) interaction. *The American Journal of Distance Education, 19*(1), 5–22. http://dx.doi.org/10.1207/s15389286ajde1901_2.

Federico, P.-A. (2000). Learning styles and student attitudes toward various aspects of network-based instruction. *Computers in Human Behavior, 16*(4), 359–379. http://dx.doi.org/10.1016/S0747-5632(00)00021-2.

Fosmire, M., & Radcliffe, D. F. (2014). *Integrating information into the engineering design process.* West LaFayette, IN: Purdue University Press.

Garritano, J. (2014). Make dependable decisions. In M. Fosmire & D. F. Radcliffe (Eds.), *Integrating Information Into The Engineering Design Process* (pp. 137–148). West LaFayette, IN: Purdue University Press.

Ghorbani, F., & Montazer, G. A. (2015). E-learners' personality identifying using their network behaviors. *Computers In Human Behavior, 51*, 42–52. http://dx.doi.org/10.1016/j.chb.2015.04.043.

Gonzales, A. L., Hancock, J. T., & Pennebaker, J. W. (2009). Language Style Matching as a predictor of social dynamics in small groups. *Communication Research, 37*(1), 3–19. http://dx.doi.org/10.1177/0093650209351468.

Graf, S., & Kinshuk, K. (2006). Considering learning styles in learning management systems: Investigating the behavior of students in an online course. In *Paper presented at the 2006 first international workshop on semantic media adaptation and personalization (Smap'06).*

Hertel, G., Schroer, J., Batinic, B., & Naumann, S. (2008). Do shy people prefer to send e-mail? Personality effects on communication media preferences in threatening and nonthreatening situations. *Social Psychology, 39*(4), 231–243. http://dx.doi.org/10.1027/1864-9335.39.4.231.

Hill, B. D., Foster, J. D., Elliott, E. M., Shelton, J. T., McCain, J., & Gouvier, W. D. (2013). Need for cognition is related to higher general intelligence, fluid intelligence, and crystallized intelligence, but not working memory. *Journal of Research in Personality, 47*(1), 22–25. http://dx.doi.org/10.1016/j.jrp.2012.11.001.

Ireland, M. E., Slatcher, R. B., Eastwick, P. W., Scissors, L. E., Finkel, E. J., & Pennebaker, J. W. (2011). Language style matching predicts relationship initiation and stability. *Psychological Science, 22*(1), 39–44. http://dx.doi.org/10.1177/0956797610392928.

Keller, H., & Karau, S. J. (2013). The importance of personality in students' perceptions of the online learning experience. *Computers in Human Behavior, 29*(6), 2494–2500. http://dx.doi.org/10.1016/j.chb.2013.06.007.

Kotov, R., Gamez, W., Schmidt, F., & Watson, D. (2010). Linking "big" personality traits to anxiety, depressive, and substance use disorders: A meta-analysis. *Psychological Bulletin, 136*(5), 768. http://dx.doi.org/10.1037/a0020327.

Landers, R. N., & Lounsbury, J. W. (2006). An investigation of Big Five and narrow personality traits in relation to Internet usage. *Computers in Human Behavior, 22*(2), 283–293. http://dx.doi.org/10.1016/j.chb.2004.06.001.

Lawrence, D. (1999). *Teaching with confidence: A guide to enhancing teacher self-esteem*. London: Paul Chapman.

Lounsbury, J. W., Foster, N., Patel, H., Carmody, P., Gibson, L. W., & Stairs, D. R. (2012). An investigation of the personality traits of scientists versus nonscientists and their relationship with career satisfaction. *R&D Management, 42*(1), 47–59. http://dx.doi.org/10.1111/j.1467-9310.2011.00665.x.

Mairesse, F., Walker, M. A., Mehl, M. R., & Moore, R. K. (2007). Using linguistic cues for the automatic recognition of personality in conversation and text. *Journal of Artificial Intelligence Research, 30*, 457–500.

Manson, J. H., Bryant, G. A., Gervais, M. M., & Kline, M. A. (2013). Convergence of speech rate in conversation predicts cooperation. *Evolution and Human Behavior, 34*(6), 419–426. http://dx.doi.org/10.1016/j.evolhumbehav.2013.08.001.

Mark, G., & Ganzach, Y. (2014). Personality and Internet usage: A large-scale representative study of young adults. *Computers In Human Behavior, 36*, 274–281. http://dx.doi.org/10.1016/j.chb.2014.03.060.

McCarthy, B., & McCarthy, D. (2006). *Teaching around the 4MAT® cycle: Designing instruction for diverse learners with diverse learning styles*. Thousand Oaks, CA: Corwin Press.

McCrae, R. R., & Costa, P. T. (1997). Personality trait structure as a human universal. *American Psychologist, 52*(5), 509–516. http://dx.doi.org/10.1037/0003-066X.52.5.509.

National Center for Education Statistics. (2016). *Digest of education statistics, 2015*. Retrieved from http://nces.ed.gov/pubsearch/pubsinfo.asp?pubid=2016014.

Nelson, M. S. (2014). Find the real need. In M. Fosmire & D. F. Radcliffe (Eds.), *Integrating information into the engineering design process* (pp. 87–100). West Lafayette, IN: Purdue University Press.

Novicki, A. (2016). *Introverts can thrive with group work*. Retrieved from https://cit.duke.edu/blog/2016/01/introverts-thrive-with-group-work/.

Park, H. S., Baker, C., & Lee, D. W. (2008). Need for cognition, task complexity, and job satisfaction. *Journal of Management in Engineering, 24*(2), 111–117. http://dx.doi.org/10.1061/(ASCE)0742-597X(2008)24:2(111).

Pavalache-Ilie, M., & Cocorada, S. (2014). Interactions of students' personality in the online learning environment. *Procedia-Social and Behavioral Sciences, 128*, 117–122. http://dx.doi.org/10.1016/j.sbspro.2014.03.128.

Pennebaker, J. W. (2011). The secret life of pronouns. *New Scientist, 211*(2828), 42–45. http://dx.doi.org/10.1016/S0262-4079(11)62167-2.

Pennebaker, J. W., Booth, R. J., & Francis, M. E. (2001). *Operator's manual Linguistic Inquiry and Word Count: LIWC 2001.* Mahwah, NJ: Erlbaum.

Pennebaker, J. W., & King, L. A. (1999). Linguistic styles: Language use as an individual difference. *Journal of Personality and Social Psychology, 77*(6), 1296. http://dx.doi.org/10.1037/0022-3514.77.6.1296.

Prince, M. (2004). Does active learning work? A review of the research. *Journal of Engineering Education, 93*(3), 223–231. http://dx.doi.org/10.1002/j.2168-9830.2004.tb00809.x.

Pritchard, P. A. (2010). The embedded science librarian: Partner in curriculum design and delivery. *Journal of Library Administration, 50*(4), 373–396. http://dx.doi.org/10.1080/01930821003667054.

Radford, A. W. (2011). *Learning at a distance: Undergraduate enrollment in distance education courses and degree programs.* US Department of Education.

Richardson, J., & Swan, K. (2003). Examining social presence in online courses in relation to students' perceived learning and satisfaction. *Jaln, 7*(1), 68–88.

Sadowski, C. J., & Cogburn, H. E. (1997). Need for cognition in the Big Five factor structure. *Journal of Psychology, 131*(3), 307–312. http://dx.doi.org/10.1080/00223989709603517.

Santo, S. A. (2006). Relationships between learning styles and online learning. *Performance Improvement Quarterly, 19*(3), 73–88. http://dx.doi.org/10.1111/j.1937-8327.2006.tb00378.x.

Schmitt, D. P., Allik, J., McCrae, R. R., & Benet-Martinez, V. (2007). The geographic distribution of Big Five personality traits: Patterns and profiles of human self-description across 56 nations. *Journal of Cross-Cultural Psychology, 38*(2), 173–212. http://dx.doi.org/10.1177/0022022106297299.

Smith, W., Sekar, S., & Townsend, K. 2002. The impact of surface and reflective teaching and learning on student academic success. *Paper presented at the learning styles: Reliability and validity: Proceedings of the 7th annual european learning styles information network conference, 26–28 June Ghent.*

Terrell, S. R. (2002). The effect of learning style on doctoral course completion in a web-based learning environment. *The Internet and Higher Education, 5*(4), 345–352. http://dx.doi.org/10.1016/S1096-7516(02)00128-8.

Vella, L. (2015). Using minute papers to determine student cognitive development levels. *Issues in Science and Technology Librarianship.*

Williamson, J. M., Lounsbury, J. W., & Han, L. D. (2013). Key personality traits of engineers for innovation and technology development. *Journal of Engineering and Technology Management, 30*(2), 157–168. http://dx.doi.org/10.1016/j.jengtecman.2013.01.003.

York, A. C., & Vance, J. M. (2009). Taking library instruction into the online classroom: Best practices for embedded librarians. *Journal of Library Administration, 49*(1–2), 197–209. http://dx.doi.org/10.1080/01930820802312995.

CHAPTER 9

Self-Reflection as a Way of Improving Instruction

9.1 SELF-REFLECTION BASED ON THE IPIP-NEO

Since reflection has increasingly been seen as important for improving instruction in the library literature (Booth, 2011), it makes sense that the librarian will want to incorporate reflection about the impact of his or her personality traits on instruction.

While personality and learning styles tests such as the 16PF and Kolb Learning Styles Inventory have a fee associated with them, the librarian can take tests available at the International Personality Item Pool (http://ipip.ori.org/) for free. The IPIP-NEO measures the Big Five personality traits and has automatic scoring (http://www.personal.psu.edu/%7Ej5j/IPIP/). There is a short version that takes 10–20 minutes and a somewhat more reliable version that takes 30–40 minutes. This section shows how to use results from the short form of the IPIP-NEO as a tool for self-reflection. Let us suppose that the librarian was given the following results from the IPIP-NEO. What instructional strengths and weaknesses would he or she have, and how might he or she improve instruction? Excerpts from the report follow.

The report begins with general guidelines about interpreting the test scores.

Please keep in mind that "low," "average," and "high" scores on a personality test are neither absolutely good nor bad. A particular level on any trait will probably be neutral or irrelevant for a great many activities, be helpful for accomplishing some things, and detrimental for accomplishing other things. As with any personality inventory, scores and descriptions can only approximate an individual's actual personality. High and low score descriptions are usually accurate, but average scores close to the low or high boundaries might misclassify you as only average. On each set of six subdomain scales it is somewhat uncommon but certainly possible to score high in some of the subdomains and low in the others. In such cases more attention should be paid to the subdomain scores than to the broad domain score. Questions about the accuracy of your results are best resolved by showing your report to people who know you well. …

Teaching to Individual Differences in Science and Engineering Librarianship
http://dx.doi.org/10.1016/B978-0-08-101881-1.00009-1

9.1.1 Extraversion

Next, the report defines Extraversion.

Extraversion is marked by pronounced engagement with the external world. Extraverts enjoy being with people, are full of energy, and often experience positive emotions. They tend to be enthusiastic, action-oriented, individuals who are likely to say "Yes!" or "Let's go!" to opportunities for excitement. In groups they like to talk, assert themselves, and draw attention to themselves.

Introverts lack the exuberance, energy, and activity levels of extraverts. They tend to be quiet, low-key, deliberate, and disengaged from the social world. Their lack of social involvement should <u>not</u> be interpreted as shyness or depression; the introvert simply needs less stimulation than an extravert and prefers to be alone. The independence and reserve of the introvert is sometimes mistaken as unfriendliness or arrogance. In reality, an introvert who scores high on the agreeableness dimension will not seek others out but will be quite pleasant when approached.

Next, the report gives the individual's overall score on Extraversion and what it means.

Your score on Extraversion is low, indicating you are introverted, reserved, and quiet. You enjoy solitude and solitary activities. Your socializing tends to be restricted to a few close friends.

9.1.2 Extraversion Facets

The report next defines the facets of Extraversion and the individuals' scores on these.

Friendliness. Friendly people genuinely like other people and openly demonstrate positive feelings toward others. They make friends quickly and it is easy for them to form close, intimate relationships. Low scorers on Friendliness are not necessarily cold and hostile, but they do not reach out to others and are perceived as distant and reserved. Your level of friendliness is average.

Gregariousness. Gregarious people find the company of others pleasantly stimulating and rewarding. They enjoy the excitement of crowds. Low scorers tend to feel overwhelmed by, and therefore actively avoid, large crowds. They do not necessarily dislike being with people sometimes, but their need for privacy and time to themselves is much greater than for individuals who score high on this scale. Your level of gregariousness is low.

Assertiveness. High scorers Assertiveness like to speak out, take charge, and direct the activities of others. They tend to be leaders in groups. Low scorers tend not to talk much and let others control the activities of groups. Your level of assertiveness is low.

Activity Level. Active individuals lead fast-paced, busy lives. They move about quickly, energetically, and vigorously, and they are involved in many activities.

People who score low on this scale follow a slower and more leisurely, relaxed pace. Your activity level is low.

Excitement-Seeking. *High scorers on this scale are easily bored without high levels of stimulation. They love bright lights and hustle and bustle. They are likely to take risks and seek thrills. Low scorers are overwhelmed by noise and commotion and are adverse to thrill-seeking. Your level of excitement-seeking is low.*

Cheerfulness. *This scale measures positive mood and feelings, not negative emotions (which are a part of the Neuroticism domain). Persons who score high on this scale typically experience a range of positive feelings, including happiness, enthusiasm, optimism, and joy. Low scorers are not as prone to such energetic, high spirits. Your level of positive emotions is average.*

9.1.3 Agreeableness

The report goes on to define Agreeableness and gives the individual's score on this trait.

Agreeableness reflects individual differences in concern with cooperation and social harmony. Agreeable individuals value getting along with others. They are therefore considerate, friendly, generous, helpful, and willing to compromise their interests with others! Agreeable people also have an optimistic view of human nature. They believe people are basically honest, decent, and trustworthy.

Disagreeable individuals place self-interest above getting along with others. They are generally unconcerned with others' well-being, and therefore are unlikely to extend themselves for other people. Sometimes their skepticism about others' motives causes them to be suspicious, unfriendly, and uncooperative.

Agreeableness is obviously advantageous for attaining and maintaining popularity. Agreeable people are better liked than disagreeable people. On the other hand, agreeableness is not useful in situations that require tough or absolute objective decisions. Disagreeable people can make excellent scientists, critics, or soldiers.

Your high level of Agreeableness indicates a strong interest in others' needs and well-being. You are pleasant, sympathetic, and cooperative.

9.1.4 Agreeableness Facets

Next, the report explains the Agreeableness facets and gives the individual's score.

Trust. *A person with high trust assumes that most people are fair, honest, and have good intentions. Persons low in trust see others as selfish, devious, and potentially dangerous. Your level of trust is high.*

Morality. *High scorers on this scale see no need for pretense or manipulation when dealing with others and are therefore candid, frank, and sincere. Low scorers believe that a certain amount of deception in social relationships is necessary. People find it relatively easy to relate to the straightforward high-scorers on this scale. They* *generally find it more difficult to relate to the unstraightforward low-scorers on this scale. It should be made clear that low scorers are <u>not</u> unprincipled or immoral; they are simply more guarded and less willing to openly reveal the whole truth. Your level of morality is high.*

Altruism. *Altruistic people find helping other people genuinely rewarding. Consequently, they are generally willing to assist those who are in need. Altruistic people find that doing things for others is a form of self-fulfillment rather than self-sacrifice. Low scorers on this scale do not particularly like helping those in need. Requests for help feel like an imposition rather than an opportunity for self-fulfillment. Your level of altruism is average.*

Cooperation. *Individuals who score high on this scale dislike confrontations. They are perfectly willing to compromise or to deny their own needs in order to get along with others. Those who score low on this scale are more likely to intimidate others to get their way. Your level of cooperation is high.*

Modesty. *High scorers on this scale do not like to claim that they are better than other people. In some cases this attitude may derive from low self-confidence or self-esteem. Nonetheless, some people with high self-esteem find immodesty unseemly. Those who <u>are</u> willing to describe themselves as superior tend to be seen as disagreeably arrogant by other people. Your level of modesty is average.*

Sympathy. *People who score high on this scale are tenderhearted and compassionate. They feel the pain of others vicariously and are easily moved to pity. Low scorers are not affected strongly by human suffering. They pride themselves on making objective judgments based on reason. They are more concerned with truth and impartial justice than with mercy. Your level of tender-mindedness is high.*

9.1.5 Conscientiousness

The report next gives a definition of Conscientiousness and the individual's score.

Conscientiousness concerns the way in which we control, regulate, and direct our impulses. Impulses are not inherently bad; occasionally time constraints require a snap decision, and acting on our first impulse can be an effective response. Also, in times of play rather than work, acting spontaneously and impulsively can be fun. Impulsive individuals can be seen by others as colorful, fun-to-be-with, and zany.

Nonetheless, acting on impulse can lead to trouble in a number of ways. Some impulses are antisocial. Uncontrolled antisocial acts not only harm other members of society, but also can result in retribution toward the perpetrator of such impulsive acts. Another problem with impulsive acts is that they often produce immediate rewards but undesirable, long-term consequences. Examples include excessive socializing that leads to being fired from one's job, hurling an insult that causes the breakup of an important relationship, or using pleasure-inducing drugs that eventually destroy one's health.

Impulsive behavior, even when not seriously destructive, diminishes a person's effectiveness in significant ways. Acting impulsively disallows contemplating alternative courses of action, some of which would have been wiser than the impulsive choice. Impulsivity also sidetracks people during projects that require organized sequences of steps or stages. Accomplishments of an impulsive person are therefore small, scattered, and inconsistent.

A hallmark of intelligence, what potentially separates human beings from earlier life forms, is the ability to think about future consequences before acting on an impulse. Intelligent activity involves contemplation of long-range goals, organizing and planning routes to these goals, and persisting toward one's goals in the face of short-lived impulses to the contrary. The idea that intelligence involves impulse control is nicely captured by the term prudence, an alternative label for the Conscientiousness domain. Prudent means both wise and cautious. Persons who score high on the Conscientiousness scale are, in fact, perceived by others as intelligent.

The benefits of high conscientiousness are obvious. Conscientious individuals avoid trouble and achieve high levels of success through purposeful planning and persistence. They are also positively regarded by others as intelligent and reliable. On the negative side, they can be compulsive perfectionists and workaholics. Furthermore, extremely conscientious individuals might be regarded as stuffy and boring. Unconscientious people may be criticized for their unreliability, lack of ambition, and failure to stay within the lines, but they will experience many short-lived pleasures and they will never be called stuffy.

Your score on Conscientiousness is average. This means you are reasonably reliable, organized, and self-controlled.

9.1.6 Conscientiousness Facets

Next, the report gives explanations of the Conscientiousness facets and the person's scores on these.

Self-Efficacy. *Self-Efficacy describes confidence in one's ability to accomplish things. High scorers believe they have the intelligence (common sense), drive, and self-control necessary for achieving success. Low scorers do not feel effective, and may have a sense that they are not in control of their lives. Your level of self-efficacy is high.*

Orderliness. *Persons with high scores on orderliness are well-organized. They like to live according to routines and schedules. They keep lists and make plans. Low scorers tend to be disorganized and scattered. Your level of orderliness is low.*

Dutifulness. *This scale reflects the strength of a person's sense of duty and obligation. Those who score high on this scale have a strong sense of moral obligation. Low scorers find contracts, rules, and regulations overly confining. They are likely to be seen as unreliable or even irresponsible. Your level of dutifulness is average.*

Achievement-Striving. *Individuals who score high on this scale strive hard to achieve excellence. Their drive to be recognized as successful keeps them on track toward their lofty goals. They often have a strong sense of direction in life, but extremely high scores may be too single-minded and obsessed with their work. Low scorers are content to get by with a minimal amount of work, and might be seen by others as lazy. Your level of achievement striving is low.*

Self-Discipline. *Self-discipline-what many people call will-power-refers to the ability to persist at difficult or unpleasant tasks until they are completed. People who possess high self-discipline are able to overcome reluctance to begin tasks and stay on track despite distractions. Those with low self-discipline procrastinate and show poor follow-through, often failing to complete tasks-even tasks they want very much to complete. Your level of self-discipline is low.*

Cautiousness. *Cautiousness describes the disposition to think through possibilities before acting. High scorers on the Cautiousness scale take their time when making decisions. Low scorers often say or do first thing that comes to mind without deliberating alternatives and the probable consequences of those alternatives. Your level of cautiousness is high.*

9.1.7 Neuroticism

The report then defines Neuroticism and gives the individual's score.

Freud originally used the term neurosis to describe a condition marked by mental distress, emotional suffering, and an inability to cope effectively with the normal demands of life. He suggested that everyone shows some signs of neurosis, but that we differ in our degree of suffering and our specific symptoms of distress. Today neuroticism refers to the tendency to experience negative feelings. Those who score high on Neuroticism may experience primarily one specific negative feeling such as anxiety, anger, or depression, but are likely to experience several of these emotions. People high in neuroticism are emotionally reactive. They respond emotionally to events that would not affect most people, and their reactions tend to be more intense than normal. They are more likely to interpret ordinary situations as threatening, and minor frustrations as hopelessly difficult. Their negative emotional reactions tend to persist for unusually long periods of time, which means they are often in a bad mood. These problems in emotional regulation can diminish a neurotic's ability to think clearly, make decisions, and cope effectively with stress.

At the other end of the scale, individuals who score low in neuroticism are less easily upset and are less emotionally reactive. They tend to be calm, emotionally stable, and free from persistent negative feelings. Freedom from negative feelings does not mean that low scorers experience a lot of positive feelings; frequency of positive emotions is a component of the Extraversion domain.

Your score on Neuroticism is average, indicating that your level of emotional reactivity is typical of the general population. Stressful and frustrating situations are somewhat upsetting to you, but you are generally able to get over these feelings and cope with these situations.

9.1.8 Neuroticism Facets

Definitions for the Neuroticism facets follow along with the individual's scores.

Anxiety. *The "fight-or-flight" system of the brain of anxious individuals is too easily and too often engaged. Therefore, people who are high in anxiety often feel like something dangerous is about to happen. They may be afraid of specific situations or be just generally fearful. They feel tense, jittery, and nervous. Persons low in Anxiety are generally calm and fearless. Your level of anxiety is high.*

Anger. *Persons who score high in Anger feel enraged when things do not go their way. They are sensitive about being treated fairly and feel resentful and bitter when they feel they are being cheated. This scale measures the tendency to feel angry; whether or not the person expresses annoyance and hostility depends on the individual's level on Agreeableness. Low scorers do not get angry often or easily. Your level of anger is low.*

Depression. *This scale measures the tendency to feel sad, dejected, and discouraged. High scorers lack energy and have difficult initiating activities. Low scorers tend to be free from these depressive feelings. Your level of depression is average.*

Self-Consciousness. *Self-conscious individuals are sensitive about what others think of them. Their concern about rejection and ridicule cause them to feel shy and uncomfortable around others. They are easily embarrassed and often feel ashamed. Their fears that others will criticize or make fun of them are exaggerated and unrealistic, but their awkwardness and discomfort may make these fears a self-fulfilling prophecy. Low scorers, in contrast, do not suffer from the mistaken impression that everyone is watching and judging them. They do not feel nervous in social situations. Your level or self-consciousness is high.*

Immoderation. *Immoderate individuals feel strong cravings and urges that they have difficulty resisting. They tend to be oriented toward short-term pleasures and rewards rather than long- term consequences. Low scorers do not experience strong, irresistible cravings and consequently do not find themselves tempted to overindulge. Your level of immoderation is low.*

Vulnerability. *High scorers on Vulnerability experience panic, confusion, and helplessness when under pressure or stress. Low scorers feel more poised, confident, and clear-thinking when stressed. Your level of vulnerability is average.*

9.1.9 Openness to Experience

Finally, the report gives the definition of Openness to Experience and the person's score.

Openness to Experience describes a dimension of cognitive style that distinguishes imaginative, creative people from down-to-earth, conventional people. Open people are Intellectually curious, appreciative of art, and sensitive to beauty. They tend to be, compared to closed people, more aware of their feelings. They tend to think and act in individualistic and nonconforming ways. Intellectuals typically score high on Openness to Experience; consequently, this factor has also been called Culture or Intellect. Nonetheless, Intellect is probably best regarded as one aspect of Openness to experience. Scores on Openness to Experience are only modestly related to years of education and scores on standard intelligent tests.

Another characteristic of the open cognitive style is a facility for thinking in symbols and abstractions far removed from Concrete Experience. Depending on the individual's specific Intellectual abilities, this symbolic cognition may take the form of mathematical, logical, or geometric thinking, artistic and metaphorical use of language, music composition or performance, or one of the many visual or performing arts. People with low scores on Openness to experience tend to have narrow, common interests. They prefer the plain, straightforward, and obvious over the complex, ambiguous, and subtle. They may regard the arts and sciences with suspicion, regarding these endeavors as abstruse or of no practical use. Closed people prefer familiarity over novelty; they are conservative and resistant to change.

Openness is often presented as healthier or more mature by psychologists, who are often themselves Open to Experience. However, open and closed styles of thinking are useful in different environments. The Intellectual style of the open person may serve a professor well, but research has shown that closed thinking is related to superior job performance in police work, sales, and a number of service occupations.

Your score on Openness to Experience is high, indicating you enjoy novelty, variety, and change. You are curious, imaginative, and creative.

9.1.10 Openness Facets

Definitions of the Openness facets and the person's scores on these follow.

Imagination. *To imaginative individuals, the real world is often too plain and ordinary. High scorers on this scale use fantasy as a way of creating a richer, more interesting world. Low scorers are on this scale are more oriented to facts than fantasy. Your level of imagination is average.*

Artistic Interests. *High scorers on this scale love beauty, both in art and in nature. They become easily involved and absorbed in artistic and natural events. They are not necessarily artistically trained nor talented, although many will be. The defining features of this scale are interest in, and appreciation of natural and artificial beauty. Low scorers lack aesthetic Sensitivity and interest in the arts. Your level of artistic interests is average.*

Emotionality. *Persons high on Emotionality have good access to and awareness of their own feelings. Low scorers are less aware of their feelings and tend not to express their emotions openly. Your level of emotionality is average.*

Adventurousness. *High scorers on adventurousness are eager to try new activities, travel to foreign lands, and experience different things. They find familiarity and routine boring, and will take a new route home just because it is different. Low scorers tend to feel uncomfortable with change and prefer familiar routines. Your level of adventurousness is high.*

Intellect. *Intellect and artistic interests are the two most important, central aspects of Openness to experience. High scorers on Intellect love to play with ideas. They are open-minded to new and unusual ideas, and like to debate Intellectual issues. They enjoy riddles, puzzles, and brain teasers. Low scorers on Intellect prefer dealing with either people or things rather than ideas. They regard Intellectual exercises as a waste of time. Intellect should <u>not</u> be equated with intelligence. Intellect is an Intellectual style, not an Intellectual ability, although high scorers on Intellect score <u>slightly</u> higher than low-Intellect individuals on standardized intelligence tests. Your level of Intellect is high.*

Liberalism. *Psychological liberalism refers to a readiness to challenge authority, convention, and traditional values. In its most extreme form, psychological liberalism can even represent outright hostility toward rules, sympathy for law-breakers, and love of ambiguity, chaos, and disorder. Psychological conservatives prefer the security and stability brought by conformity to tradition. Psychological liberalism and conservatism are not identical to political affiliation, but certainly incline individuals toward certain political parties. Your level of liberalism is high.*

9.2 IMPLICATIONS FOR TEACHING

This example profile indicates that there may be several instructional strengths and weaknesses that could be exhibited by the individual. Strengths include the librarian's high levels of Intellect, Cooperation, Trust, Tender mindedness, and Self–Efficacy.

The high Intellect, not to be confused with intelligence, may motivate the librarian to learn new things and share this information with students. The librarian will be intellectually curious. The high score on Cooperation means that the librarian will not get into confrontations with students. He or she will also tend to have a trusting attitude towards students, which could be a strength. The librarian's high Tender-mindedness may make him or her sensitive to the challenges that students face. His or her high Self-Efficacy could lead to confidence with his or her abilities to solve problems.

The librarian could have some weaknesses in regard to instruction, however. He or she scores low on several facets of Extraversion, suggesting a preference for spending time by him- or herself and a possible lesser enjoyment of group interaction. Although the librarian has average Friendliness and Cheerfulness, he or she is low on Gregariousness, Activity Level, and Excitement Seeking. This could lead to lack of energy in instructional activities and unwillingness to seek out stimulation, particularly in settings with large groups of students.

In addition, the librarian scores high on two facets of Neuroticism, Anxiety and Self-Consciousness, both of which are highly relevant to instruction. The librarian could have significant anxiety about instruction, particularly if not well trained or experienced in instructional techniques. The librarian's high self-consciousness could lead him or her to feeling that he or she is being scrutinized when providing instruction. This could inhibit the librarian's delivery greatly.

The librarian's low scores on Achievement Striving and Self-Discipline, both of which are facets of Conscientiousness, could cause him or her not to work very hard to improve his or her instructional methods, particularly if not interested in doing so. He or she might also procrastinate in preparing instruction if not interested or if he or she is anxious.

Two caveats should be added to these interpretations of the librarian's scores. First, the librarian's scores are based on his or her self-perceptions. For example, if the librarian is overly critical of himself or herself, he or she may be underestimating scores on positive traits. The 16PF has an Impression Management scale that is designed to show whether individuals are presenting a highly favorable or highly negative impression of themselves (Conn & Rieke, 1994). Individuals who score very low on Impression Management may have critical self-perceptions. The test reported here does not have an impression management scale that could furnish information about this factor.

Second, becoming aware of possible negative traits may lead some librarians to feel discouraged about the potential for improving their instruction. Librarians engaging in self-reflection about their personality must realize that personality traits are just one factor in instruction. Everyone behaves in an Extraverted way in some instances and in Introverted ways at other times, for example. Personality is never the whole story, and behavior is highly malleable, even if one has personality traits that may appear to be potential weaknesses. The benefit of engaging in self-reflection about personality is that it identifies areas that can be worked on, as well as making librarians aware of strengths they may not have known about.

The librarian in this example could set a goal to work on behaviors associated with personality traits that could have particularly negative effects on instruction, such as Anxiety and Self-Consciousness. In addition, he or she could leverage strengths that he or she becomes aware of when taking the assessment, such as Self-Efficacy and Intellect.

9.3 A CASE STUDY

My own experiences with teaching a sophomore level civil engineering technical writing class illustrates the use of reflection on personality traits and learning styles to analyze and improve instruction. For the past 15 years I have taught library instruction sessions for the same civil engineering technical writing class and have used reflection on learning styles and personality traits in recent years to analyze how to make the instruction better.

After learning about the Kolb Learning Cycle and the fact that there are other learning styles than my own lecture-oriented, assimilative learning style (which combines Abstract Conceptualization and Reflective Observation), I designed a lesson plan using the 4MAT system to incorporate the Kolb learning cycle in the two sessions I was invited to teach in Fall 2015.

The class started with my asking students to write down questions they had about finding technical information. This step was supposed to establish a connection between students' own experience and the content of the library instruction. This step was supposed to correspond with Concrete Experience and Reflective Observation in Kolb's system. I answered the questions in a second class period.

The second part of the first class was a lecture on questions to ask during the process of finding technical information. It included sections on evaluating sources and keyword searching and was supposed to correspond to Abstract Conceptualization and Reflective Observation.

The third part was a chance for students to practice these skills by responding to questions about particular sources. For example, I showed an image of a webpage and asked students to state whether it was technical or not technical based on the lecture. This section of the class was supposed to correspond to Abstract Conceptualization and Active Experimentation.

In the fourth section of the class, students were asked to find a source on their own out of class and analyze whether it was technical. This was supposed to correspond to Concrete Experience and Active Experimentation.

When I reflected upon this class, it seemed to me that personality traits and learning styles contributed to the success or lack of success of various parts of the class. First, I thought that my attempt to organize the class around a theme of "questions" was unsuccessful, possibly because it did not appeal to students' high Tough-Mindedness (low Sensitivity). The questions theme was not straightforward, logical, and down-to-earth, but somewhat aesthetic and conceptual. In a later year, I dropped the questions metaphor and taught the material in a more practical, straightforward manner, and the number of consultations I got significantly increased. Since I score rather high on Sensitivity, the idea of using a theme for the class was appealing to me,[19] but I believe it was confusing and not perceived as useful or practically relevant by the students.

Second, I noted that eliciting the questions from students about questions they had about finding technical information was particularly successful. This was a minute paper activity that I suspected appealed to both Introverted and Extraverted students. It was good because it required all students to participate, thus engaging everyone in thinking about a topic especially relevant to them. When I created slides for the follow-up class, I took the questions and provided answers. This stimulated class discussion. The minute papers also most likely appealed to both active and reflective learning styles. In addition, the minute papers may have been beneficial for any students who were Apprehensive, since it allowed them to express their concerns about the process of finding technical information.

The "practice" part of the class when I displayed examples of sources on the screen and asked students whether these were technical engaged some of the students, but I had not way of telling whether there was total participation. Upon reflection, I would have done this part differently, either using Think-Pair-Shares, votes, or some other total participation technique, to make sure all students understood the class content.

In a later version of the class, I dropped many of the features of the initial 4MAT-designed class, and I had more spontaneous class discussion and requests for consultations. In this later class, I organized the class around the practical questions I had received from students in the class from the prior year, suspecting that these would be relevant for the current students, as well:

How do you know information is "technical"?
How do you find technical information?
How do you know information is good quality?
How do you understand technical information?
How do you identify what you will need to know to cite the information?

---

[19]The 4MAT system also emphasizes having an overarching concept for the class, which in this instance was "questions."

I then gave concrete, practical answers to these questions in a lecture format. I stopped to ask students if the students had any questions, and there was a lot of discussion.

I believe that this approach was effective because it established a clear connection with the experience of the students (needing to write a technical paper); was practical, rather than conceptual; and gave the students clear steps to follow (which possibly appealed to a preference for Active Experimentation). The one part that students did not seem to understand was the concept of bias, which may have been a bit abstract for the sophomore level class.

9.4 CONCLUSION

Personality and learning styles frameworks can be used fruitfully in instruction. Tests such as the freely available IPIP-NEO can allow librarians to assess strengths and weaknesses that could be germane to instruction. Similarly, thinking about how personality and learning styles factors may have influenced the success or lack of success of past classes can be useful for adapting future instruction.

REFERENCES

Booth, C. (2011). *Reflective teaching, effective learning: Instructional literacy for library educators.* Chicago, IL: American Library Association.
Conn, S. R., & Rieke, M. L. (1994). *16PF fifth edition technical manual.* Champaign, IL: Institute for Personality and Ability Testing.

CHAPTER 10

Personality and Competencies for Engineering Students and Information Literacy

The link between competencies, or Knowledge, Skills, and Abilities, and personality traits is strong. As Lounsbury and Gibson (2006) point out, personality traits reflect individuals' typical behavior, and they add predictive power beyond cognitive aptitude and ability tests. Typical behavior is strongly related to KSAs (Knowledge, Skills, and Abilities). The scales in Lounsbury and Gibson's PSI are specified to measure work-related competencies, such as Teamwork, a propensity for working in teams. These scales have significant correlations with work-related behaviors such as new learning, relationship with co-workers, quality, and ability to function under stress.

Similarly, the Big Five personality traits have been shown to be related to competencies. Hough and Ones (2001), for example, state that personality variables are useful for "predicting prosocial, good citizenship, or contextual criterion constructs" (p. 247). Compound work-related variables such as customer service orientation, are correlated with multiple Big Five traits (Agreeableness, Emotional Stability, and Conscientiousness, in this case). Hough and Ones organize personality scales from many inventories in a taxonomy of Big Five dimensions and facets. Many of the taxons have applicability in work or academic settings. For example, Hough and Ones include an Openness to Experience facet, Creativity/Innovation that brings together features such as generating ideas and being innovative.

In a similar way, competencies in accreditation and information literacy standards seem to be related to personality traits. One may analyze which personality traits are conceptually congruous with sections of documents such as the ABET engineering accreditation standard, Criterion 3 and the ACRL Framework for Information Literacy in Higher Education. Comparisons between the ABET Criterion 3 and the ACRL Science Information Literacy Standards have been made previously (Nelson & Fosmire, 2010), but no

Teaching to Individual Differences in Science and Engineering Librarianship
http://dx.doi.org/10.1016/B978-0-08-101881-1.00010-8

comparison has been made between the ABET Criterion 3 and the ACRL Framework on Information Literacy in Higher Education on the basis of congruence with personality traits. While both of these documents are from the United States, one may follow a similar process for documents from other countries such as the United Kingdom. Also, there is some overlap between competencies referenced by engineering accreditation and information literacy standards from the United Kingdom and the United States.

10.1 ABET CRITERION 3

The history of the development of ABET Criterion 3 is discussed by Naimpally, Ramachandran, and Smith (2012). This criterion includes the abilities that are desired student outcomes for the accreditation of engineering programs in the United States. As I will show, these abilities can be mapped to Lounsbury and Gibson's PSI constructs and Hough and Ones' taxonomy of personality facets, in some cases. This section analyzes the personality traits that seem to be congruous with sections (a)–(k) of the Criterion.

(a) an ability to apply knowledge of mathematics, science, and engineering
This ability is related to Lounsbury and Gibson's Tough-Mindedness scale, since applying scientific knowledge requires logical thinking. It is also related to high Reasoning on the 16PF.

(b) an ability to design and conduct experiments as well as to analyze and interpret data
I believe that this is related to high Tough-Mindedness; Reasoning; and facets of Openness enumerated by Hough and Ones, such as Intellect (working with ideas).

(c) an ability to design a system, component, or process to meet desired needs within realistic constraints such as economic, environmental, social, political, ethical, health and safety, manufacturability, and sustainability
This may be related to Creativity/Innovation, a facet of Openness to Experience included in Hough and Ones' taxonomy.

(d) an ability to function on multidisciplinary teams
This is consonant with high Teamwork (Agreeableness) (Lounsbury and Gibson, 2006).

(e) an ability to identify, formulate, and solve engineering problems
This is congruous with high Tough-Mindedness.

(f) an understanding of professional and ethical responsibility
This is related to the Conscientiousness facets in Hough and Ones' taxonomy, Dependability and Moralistic.

(g) an ability to communicate effectively

I could find no personality trait related to this competency.

(h) the broad education necessary to understand the impact of engineering solutions in a global, economic, environmental, and societal context

This is related to Curiosity/Breadth, a facet of Openness to Experience in Hough and Ones' taxonomy.

(i) a recognition of the need for, and an ability to engage in lifelong learning

This is related to Curiosity/Breadth and Intellect, both of which are facets of Openness to Experience in Hough and Ones' taxonomy. It is also related to Openness in Lounsbury and Gibson's PSI.

(j) a knowledge of contemporary issues

I could not find any personality traits related to this competency.

(k) an ability to use the techniques, skills, and modern engineering tools necessary for engineering practice.

I could not find any personality traits specifically related to this competency.

As can be seen from this analysis, traits that would seem to be consonant with abilities called for by ABET Criterion 3 are Tough-Mindedness; Reasoning; Openness and its facets Curiosity/Breadth, Creativity/Innovation, and Intellect; Teamwork/Agreeableness; and Conscientiousness facets, Dependability and Moralistic.

10.2 THE ACRL FRAMEWORK FOR INFORMATION LITERACY FOR HIGHER EDUCATION

The ACRL framework was filed in 2015. It states:

Information literacy is the set of integrated abilities encompassing the reflective discovery of information, the understanding of how information is produced and valued, and the use of information in creating new knowledge and participating ethically in communities of learning.

The framework contains six frames and associated knowledge practices and dispositions. The knowledge practices and dispositions may be linked to conceptually congruous personality traits, as was done for ABET Criterion 3.

10.2.1 Knowledge Practices for Frame 1 Authority is Constructed and Contextual

• define different types of authority, such as subject expertise (e.g., scholarship), societal position (e.g., public office or title), or special experience (e.g., participating in a historic event);

This is congruous with high Reasoning and Tough-Mindedness.

- use research tools and indicators of authority to determine the credibility of sources, understanding the elements that might temper this credibility; This is congruous with high Tough-Mindedness.
- understand that many disciplines have acknowledged authorities in the sense of well-known scholars and publications that are widely considered "standard," and yet, even in those situations, some scholars would challenge the authority of those sources;
This is congruous with the Openness facet, Complexity, in Hough and Ones' taxonomy, which has to do with a preference for complexity or cognitive complexity.
- recognize that authoritative content may be packaged formally or informally and may include sources of all media types;
I could find no personality trait associated with this knowledge practice.
- acknowledge they are developing their own authoritative voices in a particular area and recognize the responsibilities this entails, including seeking accuracy and reliability, respecting Intellectual property, and participating in communities of practice;
This is congruous with the Conscientiousness facet, Moralistic (Hough and Ones, 2001); and Self-Esteem, which is a facet of Emotional Stability.
- understand the increasingly social nature of the information ecosystem where authorities actively connect with one another and sources develop over time.
This may be congruous with Complexity, a facet of Openness to Experience.

10.2.2 Dispositions for Frame 1 Authority is Constructed and Contextual

- develop and maintain an open mind when encountering varied and sometimes conflicting perspectives;
This is congruous with high Openness and flexibility (low Conscientiousness in Lounsbury and Gibson's PSI).
- motivate themselves to find authoritative sources, recognizing that authority may be conferred or manifested in unexpected ways;
This may be congruous with having high Complexity, a facet of Openness to Experience in Hough and Ones' taxonomy.
- develop awareness of the importance of assessing content with a skeptical stance and with a self-awareness of their own biases and worldview;
This is congruous with high Tough-Mindedness and Reflective, a composite trait in Hough and Ones' taxonomy comprised of low Extraversion and high Openness to experience.

- question traditional notions of granting authority and recognize the value of diverse ideas and worldviews;
This is congruous with high Openness and facets of Openness such Complexity.
- are conscious that maintaining these attitudes and actions requires frequent self-evaluation.
This may be congruous with Reflective, a composite trait in Hough and Ones' taxonomy comprised of low Extraversion and high Openness to experience.

10.2.3 Knowledge Practices for Frame 2 Information Creation as a Process

- articulate the capabilities and constraints of information developed through various creation processes;
This is congruous with high Reasoning and Complexity, a facet of Openness to Experience.
- assess the fit between an information product's creation process and a particular information need;
This is congruous with high Reasoning and Tough-Mindedness.
- articulate the traditional and emerging processes of information creation and dissemination in a particular discipline;
I could find no personality trait associated with this knowledge practice.
- recognize that information may be perceived differently based on the format in which it is packaged;
This is congruous with high Complexity, a facet of Openness to Experience.
- recognize the implications of information formats that contain static or dynamic information;
I could find no personality trait associated with this knowledge practice.
- monitor the value that is placed upon different types of information products in varying contexts;
This is congruous with high Tough-Mindedness.
- transfer knowledge of capabilities and constraints to new types of information products;
This is congruous with high Tough-Mindedness.
- develop, in their own creation processes, an understanding that their choices impact the purposes for which the information product will be used and the message it conveys.
This may be congruous with Reflective, a composite trait composed of low Extraversion and high Openness to Experience.

10.2.4 Dispositions for Frame 2 Information Creation as a Process

- are inclined to seek out characteristics of information products that indicate the underlying creation process;
  I could find no related personality trait.
- value the process of matching an information need with an appropriate product;
  I could find no related personality trait.
- accept that the creation of information may begin initially through communicating in a range of formats or modes;
  I could find no personality trait that matched this disposition.
- accept the ambiguity surrounding the potential value of information creation expressed in emerging formats or modes;
  This is congruous with flexibility (low Conscientiousness) and high Openness.
- resist the tendency to equate format with the underlying creation process;
  I could not match a personality trait to this disposition.
- understand that different methods of information dissemination with different purposes are available for their use.
  This may be congruous with high Openness.

10.2.5 Knowledge Practices for Frame 3 Information has Value

- give credit to the original ideas of others through proper attribution and citation;
  This is congruous with high Conscientiousness, and perhaps Agreeableness.
- understand that Intellectual property is a legal and social construct that varies by culture;
  This is congruous with high scores on the Openness facet, Culture/Artistic, in Hough and Ones' taxonomy.
- articulate the purpose and distinguishing characteristics of copyright, fair use, open access, and the public domain;
  I could find no related personality trait.
- understand how and why some individuals or groups of individuals may be under-represented or systematically marginalized within the systems that produce and disseminate information;
  This is congruous with Agreeableness, particularly the facet, Nurturance in Hough and Ones' taxonomy, which has to do with empathy and altruism.
- recognize issues of access or lack of access to information sources;

This is congruous with high Agreeableness.
- decide where and how their information is published;
  This may be congruous with high Reasoning.
- understand how the commodification of their personal information and online interactions affects the information they receive and the information they produce or disseminate online;
  This is congruous with high scores on Openness facets such as Complexity.
- make informed choices regarding their online actions in full awareness of issues related to privacy and the commodification of personal information.
  I could find no related personality trait.

10.2.6 Dispositions for Frame 3 Information has Value

- respect the original ideas of others;
  This is congruous with high Conscientiousness and Agreeableness.
- value the skills, time, and effort needed to produce knowledge;
  I could find no personality trait associated with this disposition.
- see themselves as contributors to the information marketplace rather than only consumers of it;
  This is congruous with high scores on the Emotional Stability facet, Self-Esteem.
- are inclined to examine their own information privilege.
  This is congruous with high scores on the Reflective composite personality trait (Hough and Ones, 2001), composed of low Extraversion and high Openness to Experience.

10.2.7 Knowledge Practices for Frame 4 Research as Inquiry

- formulate questions for research based on information gaps or on reexamination of existing, possibly conflicting, information;
  This is congruous with high Tough-Mindedness.
- determine an appropriate scope of investigation;
  This may be congruous with high Reasoning and Tough-Mindedness.
- deal with complex research by breaking complex questions into simple ones, limiting the scope of investigations;
  This is congruous with high scores on Complexity, a facet of Openness to Experience and high Tough-Mindedness.
- use various research methods, based on need, circumstance, and type of inquiry;

I could find no personality trait associated with this knowledge practice.
- monitor gathered information and assess for gaps or weaknesses;
  This is congruous with high Tough-Mindedness.
- organize information in meaningful ways;
  This is congruous with a high degree of Order, a facet of Conscientiousness in Hough and Ones' taxonomy.
- synthesize ideas gathered from multiple sources;
  This may be congruous with high Creativity/Innovation, a facet of Openness to Experience.
- draw reasonable conclusions based on the analysis and interpretation of information.
  This is congruous with high Reasoning and Tough-Mindedness.

10.2.8 Dispositions for Frame 4 Research as Inquiry

Learners who are developing their information literate abilities
- consider research as open-ended exploration and engagement with information;
  This is congruous with flexibility (low Conscientiousness) and high Openness to Experience.
- appreciate that a question may appear to be simple but still disruptive and important to research;
  This may be congruous with high Complexity, a facet of Openness.
- value intellectual curiosity in developing questions and learning new investigative methods;
  This is congruous with high Curiosity/Breadth, a facet of Openness.
- maintain an open mind and a critical stance;
  This is congruous with high Openness to Experience and Tough-Mindedness.
- value persistence, adaptability, and flexibility and recognize that ambiguity can benefit the research process;
  This is congruous with high Persistence, a facet of Conscientiousness; and flexibility (low Conscientiousness).
- seek multiple perspectives during information gathering and assessment;
  This is congruous with high Complexity and Curiosity/Breadth, facets of Openness to Experience in Hough and Ones' taxonomy.
- seek appropriate help when needed;
  I could find no personality trait associated with this disposition.
- follow ethical and legal guidelines in gathering and using information;
  This is congruous with high Conscientiousness.

- demonstrate intellectual humility (i.e., recognize their own intellectual or experiential limitations).

This is congruous with high Modesty, a composite trait composed of low Extraversion and high Agreeableness.

10.2.9 Knowledge Practices for Frame 5 Scholarship as Conversation

Learners who are developing their information literate abilities

- cite the contributing work of others in their own information production;
  This is congruous with high Agreeableness and high Conscientiousness.
- contribute to scholarly conversation at an appropriate level, such as local online community, guided discussion, undergraduate research journal, conference presentation/poster session;
  I could find no personality trait associated with this knowledge practice.
- identify barriers to entering scholarly conversation via various venues;
  I could find no related personality trait.
- critically evaluate contributions made by others in participatory information environments;
  This is congruous with high Tough-Mindedness.
- identify the contribution that particular articles, books, and other scholarly pieces make to disciplinary knowledge;
  This is congruous with high Tough-Mindedness and high Reasoning.
- summarize the changes in scholarly perspective over time on a particular topic within a specific discipline;
  This is congruous with high Tough-Mindedness and Reasoning.
- recognize that a given scholarly work may not represent the only or even the majority perspective on the issue.
  This may be congruous with high Openness.

10.2.10 Dispositions for Frame 5 Scholarship as Conversation

Learners who are developing their information literate abilities

- recognize they are often entering into an ongoing scholarly conversation and not a finished conversation;
  This may be congruous with Flexibility (low Conscientiousness) and high Openness.
- seek out conversations taking place in their research area;
  I could find no personality trait associated with this disposition.
- see themselves as contributors to scholarship rather than only consumers of it;

This is congruous with high Self-Esteem, a facet of Emotional Stability.

- recognize that scholarly conversations take place in various venues;
  This is congruous with high Openness.
- suspend judgment on the value of a particular piece of scholarship until the larger context for the scholarly conversation is better understood;
  This is congruous with high Openness and Flexibility (low Conscientiousness).
- understand the responsibility that comes with entering the conversation through participatory channels;
  This may be congruous with high Conscientiousness or Moralistic, a facet of Conscientiousness.
- value user-generated content and evaluate contributions made by others;
  This may be congruous with high Teamwork (Agreeableness) in Lounsbury and Gibson's PSI (2006).
- recognize that systems privilege authorities and that not having a fluency in the language and process of a discipline disempowers their ability to participate and engage.
  This may be congruous with Nurturance, a facet of Agreeableness in Hough and Ones' taxonomy.

10.2.11 Knowledge Practices for Frame 6 Searching as Strategic Exploration

Learners who are developing their information literate abilities

- determine the initial scope of the task required to meet their information needs;
  This is congruous with high Tough-Mindedness and Reasoning.
- identify interested parties, such as scholars, organizations, governments, and industries, who might produce information about a topic and then determine how to access that information;
  This may be congruous with high Openness.
- utilize divergent (e.g., brainstorming) and convergent (e.g., selecting the best source) thinking when searching;
  This is congruous with high Creativity/Innovation, a facet of Openness.
- match information needs and search strategies to appropriate search tools;
  This is congruous with high Tough-Mindedness.
- design and refine needs and search strategies as necessary, based on search results;
  This may be congruous with high Creativity/Innovation and/or Tough-Mindedness.

- understand how information systems (i.e., collections of recorded information) are organized in order to access relevant information;
  This may be congruous with high scores on Order, a facet of Conscientiousness; as well as Tough-Mindedness.
- use different types of searching language (e.g., controlled vocabulary, keywords, natural language) appropriately;
  This may be congruous with high Reasoning and Tough-Mindedness.
- manage searching processes and results effectively.
  This may be congruous with Order, a facet of Conscientiousness.

10.2.12 Dispositions for Frame 6 Searching as Strategic Exploration

Learners who are developing their information literate abilities
- exhibit mental flexibility and creativity;
  This is congruous with Flexibility (low Conscientiousness); and high Creativity/Innovation, a facet of Openness.
- understand that first attempts at searching do not always produce adequate results;
  This may be congruous with high Persistence, a facet of Conscientiousness.
- realize that information sources vary greatly in content and format and have varying relevance and value, depending on the needs and nature of the search;
  I could find no related personality trait.
- seek guidance from experts, such as librarians, researchers, and professionals;
  This may be congruous with Trust, a composite trait composed of high Emotional Stability and Agreeableness.
- recognize the value of browsing and other serendipitous methods of information gathering;
  This may be congruous with high Openness.
- persist in the face of search challenges and know when they have enough information to complete the information task.
  This is congruous with Persistence, a facet of Conscientiousness; and Tough-Mindedness.

The personality traits related to the Framework's Knowledge Practices and Dispositions thus include some of the same traits associated with the ABET standards (Openness and its facets Curiosity/Breadth and Creativity/Innovation; facets of Conscientiousness such as Moralistic; Reasoning; Teamwork (Agreeableness); and Tough-Mindedness). However, it also is associated with a number of traits not related to the ABET standards: the Emotional Stability facet, Self-Esteem; Openness facets, Complexity and Culture; high and low Conscientiousness; Agreeableness and its facet, Nurturance; the Conscientiousness facets, Order and Persistence; and the composite traits, Reflective, Modesty, and Trust. Because some of the traits that are associated with the Framework are not typical of engineers and scientists, one wonders if it would be particularly difficult to instill the knowledge practices and dispositions associated with these traits.

10.3 CONCLUSION

The ACRL Framework for Information Literacy in Higher Education is a complex document that includes knowledge practices and dispositions congruous with a wide range of personality traits. The ABET Accreditation Standards Criterion 3 appears to be congruous with some personality traits that are also associated with the Framework, although it does not seem to be related to other traits aligned with Framework. It will be interesting to see if encouraging engineering students to develop knowledge practices and dispositions from the Framework will pose any difficulties in areas that do not overlap between the two documents.

REFERENCES

Hough, L., & Ones, D. (2001). The structure, measurement, validity, and use of personality variables in industrial, work, and organizational psychology. In N. Anderson, D. Ones, & H. K. Sinagil (Eds.), *Handbook of industrial, work, and organizational psychology Volume 1: Personnel psychology* (pp. 233–277). London: SAGE.
Lounsbury, J. W., & Gibson, L. W. (2006). *Personal style inventory: A personality measurement system for work and school settings.* Knoxville, TN: Resource Associates.
Naimpally, A. V., Ramachandran, H., & Smith, C. (2012). *Lifelong learning for engineers and scientists in the information age.* London: Elsevier.
Nelson, M. S., & Fosmire, M. (2010). *Engineering librarian participation in technology curricular redesign: Lifelong learning, information literacy, and ABET Criterion 3.* Paper presented at the American Society For Engineering Education.

CHAPTER 11

Conclusion

11.1 PRACTICAL CONSIDERATIONS

What is the librarian to do when faced with the typical challenges presented by contexts of library instruction such as large class sizes, diverse audiences, "one-shot" classes in which they do not have knowledge of students' characteristics, and time constraints? Given these challenges, how can the librarian ever effectively connect with students by taking into account personality traits and learning styles? What would be the point of adding on adaptations to individual differences when the librarian is already so busy?

11.1.1 Large Classes

Some respondents to the survey mentioned that large class sizes prevented their adapting instruction to personality traits and learning styles of students. Certainly large class sizes introduce problems with eliciting total participation in class discussions, group work, and hands-on activities. In some engineering classes I have taught there have been more than 100 students, and I have been tempted to teach solely in a lecture format, rather than incorporate any interactive activities that could have created more engagement.

Teaching solely in a lecture format turns students into passive receivers of information; however, and it is a format that tends to appeal more to learners who prefer Reflective Observation rather than Active Experimentation. In addition, giving lectures to large audiences typically does not give the librarian feedback about how the instruction is going, unless he or she has also incorporated assessment activities. If the assessment is at the end of the class period, the librarian does not have the opportunity to adapt during the instructional moment.

In my opinion, three activities are useful in engaging students with diverse personality characteristics and learning styles in large classes. Think-Share-Pairs can easily be incorporated in large classes, and they should appeal to both Introverted and Extraverted students, as I discussed earlier. Think-Share-Pairs do not present many logistical problems, since the student can simply turn to the student next to himself or herself and discuss

*Teaching to Individual Differences in Science and
Engineering Librarianship*
http://dx.doi.org/10.1016/B978-0-08-101881-1.00011-X
159

the question raised by the librarian. They also do not have to take a great deal of time. I have found that Think-Share-Pairs stimulate lively discussion and create a favorable class climate. More students report on their discussions in pairs than they would if simply asked their individual thoughts on a topic. Also, the students at least have the chance to discuss the topic with the other member of their pair, even if they do not choose to report on the discussion to the larger group.

Another activity that I believe can easily be incorporated in large classes is minute papers, which are also known as Quick-Writes (Himmele & Himmele, 2011). When students do minute papers, they are asked a question and given a brief time to write. Often there is a class discussion afterwards in which some students can volunteer what they have written. Minute papers can give the librarian very valuable feedback about students' information literacy skills and the techniques they use in finding information. One example of a minute paper I assigned in a Materials Science class was asking the students to draw the process they used in finding information. This elicited flow charts showing specific sources the students used as well as some more general conceptual drawings of the information search process.

Minute papers should appeal both to Introverts and Extraverts, if time for sharing is provided after the writing so that Extraverts can participate in a way they enjoy. Minute papers can also involve logical analysis, appealing to students who are high on Tough-Mindedness (or perhaps low on Sensitivity). It can also appeal to students who are creative (high on Openness facets and low on Conscientiousness). Minute papers can be appealing to both active and reflective learners, as well, since it involves reflection and producing an output (the paper). Minute papers are great for large classes because they do not present any logistical challenges.

A third activity that is good for large classes and can appeal to both Introverted and Extraverted students is voting, which can be done either by clickers or a show of hands. Using clickers would allow more anonymity for students who are low on Emotional Stability, low on Social Boldness, or high on Apprehension. However, clickers do present a logistical challenge for librarians teaching large classes, since not all engineering or science classes require the students to be equipped for an audience response system.

11.1.2 Diverse Audiences

Some respondents to the survey pointed out that students have diverse characteristics in any class. I agree with this and realize that this poses some problems for using the stereotypical profile approach (i.e., attempting to appeal to the predominant personality or learning style characteristics of students in a class, based on knowledge of the typical traits of engineers and scientists). If time permits, the librarian can provide well-balanced instruction incorporating activities appealing to a variety of different learners.

The librarian could also focus on providing instruction using activities congruous with the content. As I mentioned earlier, information literacy instruction aligns with the trait of having high Openness. Other traits may be aligned with information literacy, as well, as I showed in the preceding chapter on the ACRL Information Literacy Framework for Higher Education. I believe that Openness is the trait most aligned with information literacy, because for other traits such as Conscientiousness, sometimes the low pole of the trait seems to be aligned with the framework, and sometimes the high pole. For example, low Conscientiousness (high flexibility) could be associated with parts of the framework having to do with creativity, and high Conscientiousness could be associated with parts about responsible use of information. I found no parts of the framework that seemed to be aligned with having low Openness. Openness to Change is also high in scientists and engineers, so adapting instruction to content that is congruous with high Openness could appeal to the predominant profile of STEM students, as well.

In this vein, it can be engaging to diverse audiences of engineering and science students to emphasize the useful new knowledge they can acquire by using current awareness tools like RSS feeds and databases (Kolah & Fosmire, 2010). I have found that engineering graduate students seem to enjoy learning about tools that are new to them such as ProWritingAid, Ludwig, mind mapping software, and bibliographic management software. Undergraduates fulfilling their continuing education requirements have been surprised (and I hope interested) to learn about tools such as SureChemBL.

11.1.3 Lack of Knowledge of Students' Personality Traits and Learning Styles

An objection to the idea of personalizing instruction that comes up repeatedly is the problem that in most cases one cannot know the personality traits and learning styles of students. Practically speaking, with the extremely thin slices of behavior that the librarian observes, how can he or she tailor instruction to individual differences? A pragmatic answer is that the librarian can form working hypotheses based on his or her observations and adjust to individuals with flexibility. For example, if a librarian notices that an engineering student is extremely outgoing, he or she may want to provide some opportunity for class discussion, even if it is hard to draw most of the other students out. If a librarian goes into a class and notices that hardly anyone responds to his or her greetings and casual questions before the instruction, he or she may want to assume a high degree of Introversion and low Social Boldness. To draw these students out the librarian may need to include Think-Pair-Shares, minute papers, or stimulate high engagement by connecting the instruction closely to a class assignment, if there is one.

I believe that one can be fairly certain that most engineers and scientists will display high Tough-Mindedness, simply due to the nature of their logical subject matter. The librarian can assume this trait is prevalent in a class even if he or she does not know the traits of individuals. This means the librarian may want to take a logical approach as one of the respondents to the survey did in having students analyze search results for anomalies.

The librarian can also assume high Reasoning in most students and plan to include some challenging material that makes students think. I did this in a sophomore civil engineering class when teaching them about TRB citation style when I gave them a list of references and asked them to identify what kind of documents these references were. One has to be careful not to be *too* challenging; however, keeping in mind that many sophomores are novices when it comes to information literacy skills. The highly intelligent engineering and science students at undergraduate and graduate levels will probably appreciate instruction that is not too slow. I have also found it is good in some cases to let the graduate students structure the class by providing questions they want answered.

Other traits may vary more, rather than occurring at high levels in most engineers and scientists. For example, not all engineers are going to score low in emotional stability even though the average for the group on emotional stability is lower than the norm population. One also might wonder if the librarian really needs to be concerned about low levels of emotional stability in students, since ungraded information literacy instruction would seem to be not particularly stressful. I would argue that the librarian does need to assume that some students will be prone to stress, particularly since engineering and the sciences are very challenging programs. The librarian can help these students, whose low emotional stability or high degree of stress may be invisible by creating a comfortable class climate, offering individual help with things that students typically find stressful, such as finding sources for technical papers, and generally looking for ways to help based on knowledge of the curriculum and the kinds of projects or exams the students must undertake.

11.1.4 Time Constraints

The librarian is faced with time constraints, often meeting just one time with students for less than an hour. Since there is a lot of material, is it possible to incorporate activities for all learning styles? "Teaching around the cycle" mentioned earlier has at least four components if one follows Kolb's learning cycle, and eight if one follows 4MAT (McCarthy & McCarthy, 2006). If the librarian already has several information literacy objectives to cover, how can he or she move through all four stages of the learning cycle? It would seem that the librarian would more likely have to focus on the lecture portion and perhaps some limited practice. This would mean only the Assimilation (Abstract Conceptualization and Reflective Observation) and the Converging (Abstract Conceptualization and Active Experimentation) quadrants would be addressed.

However, not all stages of the learning cycle need to be addressed within class. The librarian could add an assignment (with the faculty member's approval) for the students to email a technical source that they find and provide feedback on their search process. This would address the Accommodation quadrant (Concrete Experience with Active Experimentation). That would leave only adding to the class time a brief Diverging activity (Concrete Experience with Reflective Observation) in which the librarian establishes a connection with students by having them relate the instructional topic to their concrete experiences. Arguably providing a brief connective component like this would be worthwhile in that it could increase engagement throughout the class.

11.2 THE FUTURE OF ADAPTING TO INDIVIDUAL DIFFERENCES

Some STEM educators are becoming aware of the need for new attributes in scientists and engineers of the future. I believe that this awareness could possibly lead to changes in the average personality trait profiles of scientists and engineers discussed earlier.

Attributes desired for the engineer of 2020 according to a NAP report (National Academy of Engineering, 2005) include: strong analytical skills; practical ingenuity; creativity; communication; business and management; leadership; high ethical standards; professionalism; dynamism, agility, resilience, and flexibility; and lifelong learners. While some of these attributes have always been desirable in engineers, such as strong analytical skills, others may be new to the increasingly global, socially and economically complex, interdisciplinary, rapid context in which engineers practice.

Engineering and science educators may increasingly need to recruit some students with "atypical" traits for the average profile. For example, while high ethical standards are not necessarily lacking in all individuals with lower Rule-Consciousness, they could be more prevalent in students with higher degrees of this trait. In additional, leadership skills may come more naturally to more Extraverted or Dominant students. Resilience may come more naturally to students with higher Emotional Stability. The typical science and engineering traits of high Openness to Change and flexibility (low Conscientiousness compared to the norm population) are most likely associated with creativity, which is one of the skills seen as desirable in the NAP report. The high levels of Tough-Mindedness and Reasoning typically found already in scientists and engineers should also be associated with the desirable traits of having good analytical skills and practical ingenuity.

One may add to these desirable attributes, interpersonal skills, which may be undeveloped in some students who fit the typical profile of scientists and engineers. A *Nature* Comment article (Leiserson & McVinney, 2015) argues that science professors need leadership skills, since, to give one example, interpersonal conflicts in labs can slow down productivity. Leadership skills can also help scientists who lead labs to motivate different staff, colleagues and students and to appreciate diversity that can lead to more innovative products. As the authors state: "Engineering and science must adapt to value the quality of interpersonal relationships, which are essential to teamwork. They must respect the diversity of thought, especially nontechnical modes, if they wish to inspire creativity."

This sort of interpersonal, inclusive focus may not come naturally to those scientists and engineers who prize rational thought over emotion. Engineers' highly objective nature (low Sensitivity) may lead some of them to have difficulties with these sorts of interpersonal skills. Engineers also scored low on Teamwork (Agreeableness) on the Personal Style Inventory, as mentioned earlier. In the future, science and engineering educators may try to recruit students who display more interpersonal skills, if the interpersonal component continues to be important.

11.2.1 Development of Skills Rather than Recruitment for Attributes

Another possibility is that educators will try to develop skills associated with desirable attributes in scientists and engineers, without trying to change traits that may not be highly malleable. For example, it would perhaps be impossible to change an Introvert into an Extravert, or vice versa, but one could improve communication and leadership skills in Introverts. One way Leiserson and McVinney (2015) fostered interpersonal leadership skills in scientists who led labs was to have them role play a dispute between two students claiming first authorship. The scientists engaged in "method acting" techniques so that they could learn to empathize with the characters in the conflict scenario.

Librarians have skills that could help develop desirable behaviors in engineering students, such as interpersonal skills. One may notice similarities between the reference interview and the skills Nelson (2014) describes teaching to engineering design students in "Find the Real Need," which she points out:

> Eliciting information from the design client and other stakeholders is a significant challenge even for experienced engineers. For students, it can be highly frustrating. The challenge for the engineering designer lies in drawing out the design client's understandings and observations and comparing that information to ideas elicited from others in order to get a comprehensive picture of the existing environment, the identified problem, and the most desirable outcome. Constructing this knowledge relies heavily on communication skills, not as taught in undergraduate speech classes, but as practiced on the library reference desk and other public service points. These interactions often require extensive interaction and follow up to tease out the client's fundamental question, let alone the final answer. Most undergraduate engineering design students will need to be explicitly taught skills to enable them to perform this type of interaction (Nelson, 2009).

Nelson (2014) describes teaching about open-ended questioning, active listening, perception re-checking, and body language, all of which might come more naturally to those engineers who have high Agreeableness than those with lower scores on this trait. She also recommends that the students learning these skills be aware that individuals may have different learning and informing styles.

Librarians can also model skills associated with desirable attributes such as high ethical standards, persistence, and resilience that they can encourage students to develop. For example, librarians can model high ethical standards when discussing avoiding plagiarism. They model persistence when they remind students that information searching is a trial and error process requiring multiple attempts and patient sifting through results. Also, in individual search consultations with stressed students, librarians can give hope that technical sources will be found, which may contribute to the students' resilience.

11.3 PERSONALITY TRAITS AND LEARNING STYLES AS FRAMEWORKS FOR INSTRUCTION

Throughout this book I have attempted to convince readers that individual differences provide a fruitful perspective for analyzing, planning, and flexibly adapting instruction. At the beginning of the book I discussed how the individuals in different occupations and majors tend to have distinct average profiles of personality traits and learning styles. I have also emphasized that despite these average scores, there is a range of personality trait and learning style scores within occupational and academic specialization groups. Some engineers are Extraverted, even if the group average Extraversion score is low. Differences such as these may suit individuals to different specializations within engineering and science careers. For example, the Extraverted engineer might be designated to be in charge of interfacing with customers to determine their design product needs. Or he or she might be positioned as a project leader.

Just as there is diversity in respect to personality traits and learning styles in science and engineering students, the same is true of librarians. Each librarian will have his or her strengths and weaknesses in instruction, partially due to personality traits and his or her own learning style. The example Big Five personality profile used in the self-reflection chapter, for example, showed weaknesses in the individual such as high Self-Consciousness, but also strengths such as high Openness to Experience. Similarly, one's own learning style conveys strengths and weaknesses. A librarian who is an Assimilator may be comfortable and proficient with lecturing, but may have a hard time connecting with students with other learning styles if he or she has not learned how to do this. Kolb and Kolb's latest learning styles instrument, the KLSI 4.0, includes a learning flexibility measure so that the learner can see whether he or she switches between learning styles readily (Kolb & Kolb, 2013). Presumably librarians with higher learning flexibility could connect better with students having different learning styles than their own.

Personality traits and learning styles are thus useful in understanding students and oneself and inferring possible challenges and strengths for learning or instruction. In addition, individual difference frameworks are connected to pedagogy. The librarian can select instructional techniques aligned with particular personality traits or learning styles—or not—if the curriculum does not seem to warrant doing so, or if the students need stretch activities.

Engineering and science pedagogy has increasingly been using active learning techniques (Waldrop, 2015), which have been shown to be more effective than students' passive receiving of information in lectures that have not been designed to be interactive. If not already doing so, librarians need to incorporate active learning exercises in their instruction if possible, so as to facilitate conceptual understanding and later transfer of information literacy skills that students have learned to their lives. Teaching to learning styles ensures active learning exercises as it prompts students to engage in reflection and Active Experimentation. The reflection activities should cause students to connect deeply with the subject matter and relate it to their experiences or knowledge. The Active Experimentation activities should allow students to test out skills and apply them in real life situations.

Even if the student does not entirely master an information literacy skill during library instruction, he or she may become actively engaged with information literacy concepts when stimulated to reflect and act upon these ideas. He or she can later contact the librarian to refresh the details. Using activities suited to a range of personality trait scores, such as both high and low Extraversion, can make the active learning activities more effective.

In addition to having important connections with pedagogy, individual differences are related to the context in which the science or engineering librarian works. The librarian is guided by standards such as the ABET Criterion 3 and the ACRL Information Literacy Framework for Higher Education and most likely wants to accomplish the objectives in these documents. An analysis shows that while some of the personality traits aligned with the two guiding documents are the same, others are different. Parts of the frameworks may be differentially appealing, seeming more natural to some students than others. This is not surprising since information literacy is multifaceted, but it does show that the librarian needs to be aware how students' individual differences may be involved in receiving parts of the information literacy message. For example, a student who scores high on Tough-Mindedness might be very comfortable with the many parts of the ACRL Information Literacy Framework for Higher Education that are aligned with high values of this trait. A student who is high on Agreeableness might be more comfortable with other sections of the Framework.

Also part of the context in which the librarian works is the presence of elements such as large class sizes, limited opportunities to interact with students, and time constraints, to name a few. Despite these challenges, I believe that it is feasible and productive for the STEM librarian to incorporate an individual differences perspective in planning instruction and flexibly adapting in the instructional moment.

REFERENCES

Himmele, P., & Himmele, W. (2011). *Total participation techniques: Making every student an active learner.* Alexandria, VA: ASCD.
Kolah, D., & Fosmire, M. (2010). Information portals: A new tool for teaching information literacy skills. *Issues in Science and Technology Librarianship.*

Kolb, A. Y., & Kolb, D. A. (2013). *The Kolb Learning Style Inventory 4.0: A comprehensive guide to the theory, psychometrics, research on validity and educational applications.* Experience Based Learning Systems, Inc.

Leiserson, C. E., & McVinney, C. (2015). Science professors need leadership training. *Nature, 523*, 279–281. http://dx.doi.org/10.1038/523279a.

McCarthy, B., & McCarthy, D. (2006). *Teaching around the 4MAT® cycle: Designing instruction for diverse learners with diverse learning styles.* Thousand Oaks, CA: Corwin Press.

National Academy of Engineering. (2005). *Educating the engineer of 2020: Adapting engineering education to the new century.* Washington, DC: National Academies Press.

Nelson, M. S. (2014). Find the real need. In M. Fosmire & D. F. Radcliffe (Eds.), *Integrating Information into the Engineering Design Process* (pp. 87–100). West LaFayette, IN: Purdue University Press.

Waldrop, M. (2015). The science of teaching science. *Nature, 523*, 272–274. http://dx.doi.org/10.1038/523272a.

INDEX

Note: Page numbers followed by *t* indicate tables and *np* indicate footnote.

Printed and bound by CPI Group (UK) Ltd, Croydon, CR0 4YY

08/06/2025

01896869-0011